PRAISE FOR SOUL PROPRIETOR

Most day: _____ helmed. But wisdom and helpful sugge _____ immediately when I turn to Jane Pollak's Soul Proprietor. Inside I find great ideas and insights, presented in brief 'bites,' from someone who has 'walked the walk' of a busy entrepreneur.

— Lucy Hedrick
Author – Get Organized in the Digital Age

Being an entrepreneur can be a lonely endeavor. Having Jane's book beside you gives you inspiration, guidance, and a friend to help you live successfully as an entrepreneur.

— Barbara Weltman
Publisher of Big Ideas for Small Business®

When you're absolutely fed up with business books that speak at you instead of with you; when you're tired of reading books that don't address you as a whole person, but solely as a business owner, read this book. Soul Proprietor speaks directly to the heart of entrepreneurs everywhere and conjures in the soul something primal and passionate - the love of being in love with your business. How divine.

— Lena West
CEO & Chief Strategist at xynoMedia

Jane covers the waterfront concerning every aspect of running a small business from accounting to marketing to the business plan. From her personal experiences she reveals the joys and disappointments of being a successful small business owner. Everyone considering starting or running a small business should read this book.

— Vance Ward
SCORE – Past Chairman Fairfield County Chapter

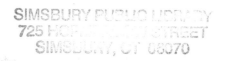

In today's highly competitive marketplace, keeping the "soul" in business can be a challenge. Jane has not only grown a company that reflects her priorities and values, but now, shares those lessons so that you too can be your own "Soul Proprietor". If you are just embarking on, or in the middle of, an entrepreneurial venture, reading and learning the lessons in Jane's book can become that "little voice" of common sense and wisdom that can guide you on your journey."

— Rebecca Surran
Anchor, News 12 Connecticut

A lifestyle entrepreneur is someone with a successful business and a meaningful personal life. Jane Pollak's excellent guide describes true-to-life issues to help you make better decisions about taking your business—and your life—to the next level.

— Susan Keane Baker
Author – Managing Patient Expectations

Jane Pollak's Soul Proprietor is not only inspiring and motivating for the entrepreneur or small business owner, it is a handbook of lessons that one could apply to the business of everyday life. Her anecdotal stories add humor and thought provoking insight into what it really takes to launch a successful business. Jane's practical wisdom and tactical strategies will help you to chart your own course for success.

— Fran Pastore
President & CEO, The Women's Business Development Center

Soul
Proprietor

101 LESSONS FROM A
LIFESTYLE ENTREPRENEUR

Jane Pollak

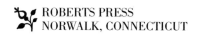

ROBERTS PRESS
NORWALK, CONNECTICUT

For information on bulk purchases or group discounts for this title, please contact our special sales director at 866.846.4345.

Library of Congress Cataloging-in-Publication Data

Pollak, Jane. 1948 –
    Soul Proprietor: 101 Lessons from a Lifestyle Entrepreneur / Jane Pollak .
        p. cm.
    Includes bibliographic references.
        ISBN 978-0-9746225-1-4
    1. New business enterprises—Management. 2. Women-owned business enterprises—Management 3. Home-based business—Management. 4. Small business—Management. 5. Entrepreneurship. I. Title.

Jane Pollak
PO Box 2605
Westport, CT 06880
www.janepollak.com
www.janepollakblog.com
jane@janepollak.com
0 9 8 7 6 5 4 3 2 1

To Laura
Who inspired my journey.

TABLE OF CONTENTS

143   CHAPTER 8

Feed Your Golden Goose – Self-Care Matters

153   CHAPTER 9

Catch the Curve Balls – Grow and Adjust Along the Way

183   CHAPTER 10

Claim the Prize – Enjoy the Rewards of Soul Proprietorship

FOREWORD

I'm not sure when I first realized that what my mom was doing in our family room, in sweatpants and sneakers, while my younger siblings and I watched *You Can't Do That on Television* in the next room, was actually a business.

I do know that it was hard to explain to other kids.

Now, of course, we know that what our mom was doing was building a soul proprietorship—a business that allowed and continues to allow her to work from home, wear sweatpants (although she's a lot more chic now), and maintain a balance of self, work, and family. Although there was no existing career path for an Egg Decorator/Small Business Coach/Professional Speaker, she chose to follow her interests and create a business—and a life—that made her happy and fulfilled.

It's a choice that more and more women and men are making these days. According to the Center for Women's Business Research, there are more than 10.1 million women-owned businesses in the United States today, and that number is growing at twice the rate of male-owned businesses. IRS statistics show that sole proprietorships in general have been on the rise since 2006. And, according to the U.S. Small Business Administration, the number of self-employed Americans ages fifty-five to sixty-four is soaring, climbing fifty-two percent from 2000 to 2007. Thanks to growing opportunities in Web-based businesses such as blogs, eBay and Etsy, and a new generation of tech-savvy young people joining the workforce, the ranks of small-business owners are sure to continue to grow and diversify.

It would be a daughter's boasting to say my mom sparked this trend from our downstairs family room. But it's accurate to say that Jane Pollak has, over the past three decades, inspired and motivated thousands of people to consider and pursue entrepreneurial lives. As you'll discover on the pages to come, she's done that through her own unique blend of "soul" and "proprietorship."

On the "soul" front, Jane has the ability to open up about her life and work in a way that helps others feel more comfortable and less afraid. It's rare to find a successful person who is so willing to share and draw lessons from her own struggles.

On the "proprietor" side of things, Jane has built an enduring, profitable business without any formal training or corporate experience. She is an example of how persistence, hard work, and a willingness to learn can turn anyone into a CEO. And she is more than willing to share everything she's gleaned over the years with the women she coaches and the readers of her blog and this book.

If you hadn't guessed already, you won't be surprised to learn that I am among the many people inspired to entrepreneurship by Jane Pollak. For the past ten years, I've run my own business as an author, speaker, and consultant for young professionals. I'm proud to say my mom has been an advisor and cheerleader—as she will be yours—every step of the way.

On behalf of my brother, Rob, and sister, Laura, I am honored to introduce you to our mother, Jane Pollak. I envy you the joy of being able to hear her stories and advice for the first time.

Lindsey Pollak
March 2010
New York City

INTRODUCTION

I am often asked if I am still decorating eggs, the craft I pursued for thirty years. The answer is "No." If pressed for details, I list the signals the universe sent me to indicate that this part of my career was over:

- The two sisters-in-law who sold me the beautiful white Pekin duck eggs for my jewelry went through messy divorces and ceased caring for the ducks that laid these treasured shells.
- Myron Surmach, whose store sold me all of my egg-decorating supplies, died of a heart attack, leaving me without a primary cheerleader and advocate.
- A catalog that featured my work prominently overpriced my eggs ($480 each) and failed to reap a profit from them, leading to their disappointment and mine.
- And finally, the week I was supposed to be on *The Martha Stewart Show* was the week she went to jail.

Had all these occurred in the first few years of my business, I would have considered them challenges and eagerly pursued new resources and opportunities. But after thirty years, I felt that artistically I had already said everything in eggs I needed to say. The speaking and coaching parts of my business were growing, and I wanted to pay more attention to them. I knew I had to let go of something.

I was born to be a life coach. The thing is, the industry didn't come into existence until the middle of my career. As it turned out, I needed all those years as an egg decorator/craft artist and speaker to enlighten me and prepare me for my ultimate calling. The lessons I learned from 1973 to 2003 were hard won and have stayed with me. There continue to be new lessons to learn, many of which are included in this new edition of *Soul Proprietor*. I plan to keep learning.

A few years ago, I attended a seminar offered by Ladies Who Launch, an organization devoted to helping entrepreneurial women. Two women who had recently sold their company for several million dollars discussed the contrast between their business and a lifestyle business. "We formed this company for the express purpose of creating an entity that we could sell for a lot of money. The product was something we were interested in, but that was not the driving force. Making a lot of money was our goal."

"A lifestyle business," one co-owner added, "is not created to be sold. It is designed to support the business owner and allow that person to pursue a passion throughout her life."

Not only was this a clear explanation, but it also illustrated something I'll always remember. There wasn't one thing about the story of their successful *non*-lifestyle business that touched my heart. There was no passion to be seen, no joy in the process. The anecdotes leading up to the sale of their business were filled with unpleasant details and activities I would never want to endure no matter how much money I could make. Like the day one co-owner's second husband came home and asked for a divorce. Their story crystallized for me why I do what I do.

I love my work. I love each day. I love my life. My bottom line, like theirs, is also black. And my heart and soul are constantly filled with joy and purpose.

※　※　※

CHAPTER 1

Align Your Course
with Your Purpose

My friend Steve teasingly dubbed me the cave painter of White Plains, New York, when I told him of my artistic beginnings, making crayon drawings on the basement walls. I was fortunate to have my talent and passion recognized early by my parents. "You got to be the artist," my older sister, the writer, said somewhat jealously in our adulthood.

After putting in a brief stint as an office temp in a boring corporate shipping department during a college break, I knew I'd never be a 9-to-5'er. Even teaching in a public school was claustrophobic for me. I needed to set my own course, doing my own work at my own pace.

Over my long career, I have come to appreciate that my quintessential gift is creative, but no longer as an artist. Throughout my career, one path I have consistently navigated is educating myself and then passing on that wisdom to others. The course has been demanding and uneven, but the direction has been guided by my spirit and always will be.

LESSON 1
The business plan is not as important as the process of creating it.

As a child, I believed that if you were truly grown-up, you would know how to speak French and how to drive a car with a stick shift. I thought that the rite of passage to adulthood was restricted to people with these skills. Similarly, as a young entrepreneur, I believed that having a business plan was the great delineator between dilettantes and successful business owners. I was a dilettante. Not that I wasn't successful—I just didn't feel legitimate or grown-up as an owner of a business, and when anyone asked me if I had a business plan, I dodged the issue by saying, "Sure—it's in my head." My plan was to make more money. My method was to participate in more shows. I had never taken the time to go beyond these two statements.

I was in business for more than ten years before I had to do a business plan as homework for a course I was taking. I had to shut down my operations for a day or two and go through this lengthy, sometimes boring process, not knowing what the outcome would be. Although writing a business plan is pretty much a matter of filling in the blanks of a formula, it is not easy. Many of the empty spaces require a great deal of thought. I gained new insights and came to new conclusions as I went through the process.

First I had to write a description of my business. I used to stammer in response to the question "What do you do?" As simple and straightforward as that question was, it required massive thought to say succinctly how I spent the major part of my working day.

Creating a goal or mission statement also took time. What sentence would inspire me when I lost my way, drive me to loftier goals, and keep me true to myself as an entrepreneur and human being?

Evaluating my market and competitors helped me establish guidelines for reaching my customers. Although my art form was distinctive, I had been exhibiting amid 100 or more artists who also produced unique treasures. While some shoppers were there solely to buy a pair of my earrings, most people came to craft shows looking for something "special." I realized I needed to create venues where everyone came to see just me. Sales held in my studio proved to be a lucrative and rewarding alternative.

Listing staff is another part of the business plan. I hadn't really regarded the high school girls who worked in my studio after school as personnel. That sounded so . . . formal. But they were on my payroll and had to be considered employees. Another new perception. Another notch on my entrepreneurial belt.

Describing my operations and production was straightforward. I listed the computer and printer, the copier and fax machine, plus all of the tools and machinery I'd acquired specifically for my craft. The whole list took up nearly two pages. "Hmm," I thought, "this is pretty impressive stuff."

After I had finished doing the business plan, I felt as though I'd been put through a wringer. I didn't look any different after creating the plan, but something inside had shifted. I shared my plan with my classmates. No one else had completed the assignment, and the whole class regarded me with awe. I, too, was awed. The process of self-examination, thought, and articulation had transformed me. No, it didn't bring me instant success. It did provide me with a foundation that led to future success. Yes, a business plan is wonderful, it will make the navigation easier, but it isn't the journey. Learning how your business's gears work is life-altering.

※　※　※

LESSON 2
Create a résumé as though you are applying for a job. You'll be impressed by who you are.

When my children were very young, I used to pore over the classified ads. I can see now that I was tempted, I wanted to look for a way to escape my life as a stay-at-home mother. I thought that if I could pull in a big salary, I could rationalize leaving the nest.

Before I became a mother, I was a high school art teacher. After that, I kept my hand in the art world by exhibiting my work once or twice a year and teaching art classes in my home. But it was hard to work, moving all the toys to transform the play area into an art studio/classroom twice a week. And having eight more children drawing and painting in my house was exhausting. A job outside the home seemed particularly glamorous.

One day an ad caught my eye. A company wanted someone with art experience and a degree in education. I thought, "Perfect! I'm it!" The salary was $40,000, a hefty sum back then. It would justify my exit from full-time motherhood. I pictured myself going to the interview in a stylish new suit and pumps, impressing my interviewers with my expertise.

Because I had been out of the job market for many years, I thought it would be prudent to get help with my résumé. I met a counselor at my alma mater and described my situation—at home with three children, running an art program, and exhibiting my work at craft shows. "Why on earth do you want to leave such a good life?" she said. She was envious that I was able to work part time and be at home with my three children. She made it seem that I had what everyone wanted. I never thought that what I had at home was so special.

However, I still wanted to pursue the administrative job, and she helped me write my résumé. Actually, she transformed my credentials into something remarkable—a technique I have adopted in my business. "In addition to your craft work, what else have you been doing in the art field since you had children?" she asked. "Oh, I started having some kids come over to my house after school to help them with their drawing and painting." She translated it: "You run a community-based art program." My self-esteem began to rise. "I won a blue ribbon at a local craft fair." "Award-winning artist," she wrote in my file. My heavens, my spirit soared. She's right. I really do have an exciting life.

I believe the universe supplies us with everything we need for our growth, including stones we use to step on and rocks we stumble over. The meeting with that counselor helped me understand what I already had and what I valued most.

Luckily, I never made it to the interview stage for that job.

※   ※   ※

LESSON 3

Writing down your goals is the beginning of the transformation process.

"I'm going to be an author when I grow up because I love books. I want to go to Mount Holyoke College. I'm going to marry a millionaire and have a mink coat and lots of jewels. When I get married I'm going to have two children."

Written in the hand of an eight-year-old, this crayon-illustrated essay on lined paper hangs in my friend Aimee's loft in Manhattan. She lives there with her millionaire husband, Joe, and two daughters, Louisa and Emma. She has written a 300-page novel and is working on a second. Aimee and I have been friends since 1967, when we met in an introductory theater arts course in college. I've taken two courses in goal setting, but never was the power of the written goal evidenced more clearly than with Aimee's framed commitment from thirty-plus years ago—before most people were even talking about goal setting.

When Laura, my youngest child, was three years old, I signed up for a weekend workshop on goal setting. It was a luxurious opportunity to delve into my heart's desires. I had two days to be introspective, to dream big dreams, and to understand the principles of laying out goals for myself. I had begun listening to audiotapes that motivated me to take a closer look at my life. *Choosing Your Own Greatness* by Wayne Dyer and *You Can Make Your Life an Adventure* by Roger Dawson are two that had a major impact on my outlook and attitude.

One of the exercises we had to do at that workshop was to set a long-term goal. It was a chance to take a good, long look ahead, to consider what we'd like to be doing in a year, three years, ten or more years. Since my three children were all under ten at the time, I had not yet looked past PTA meetings and volunteerism. What the heck, I thought, why not create a wish list? What's the harm? I wrote down that in ten to fifteen years I wanted to be a motivational speaker. I wanted to change people's lives the way Wayne Dyer and Roger Dawson had changed mine. I had no area of expertise to speak about. I had no message and I had no audience in mind. Still, I wrote down that goal.

The instructor at the workshop taught me that something physiological happens when the eye sees the hand writing a message. Writing "I want to be a motivational speaker" and then seeing the words on paper gave me an immediate rush of adrenaline, and my heart started to beat faster.

I made the decision to take my business to a new level. I put in more hours working on my egg decorating, trying new designs, gaining expertise in my craft. Several years later, when my youngest child was nine and we had put away most of the toys, my husband and I converted our family room into a quasi-home office. We shared the space, a computer, and a copier. To become more successful, I needed to become more productive. To become more productive, I was going to need a more efficiently designed space. I set the goal to convert our newly created home office into a studio for my business.

No sooner had I committed the goal to paper than I attended a luncheon for my Entrepreneurial Woman's Network and found myself seated next to an architectural designer who had her portfolio with her. I was able to look at it, and what at first appeared to be an overwhelming project—remodeling the family room—became manageable with her expertise. My renovated studio was completed in less than seven months.

The new space changed more than my productivity. It enhanced my self-image. Now I felt I could invite customers over, hold studio sales, and enjoy being photographed there. Sales and income increased, and I began to realize that I was achieving at a higher level as a result of remodeling.

Incrementally I was taking the steps necessary to become a motivational speaker. I was developing expertise in entrepreneurship so that other people would be interested to hear how I did it. It would be true to say that I wrote down long-term goals and achieved them. But the transformation was slow, step by step, inch by inch. Writing down my goals began the process.

※　※　※

LESSON 4
Make sure your business suits your ever-changing lifestyle.

When some people leave their corporate jobs, they already know they're going to start their own business. While still on the payroll, they researched the industry they were planning to enter, created a business plan, and found their office space; only then, they hung out their shingle.

Then there's the rest of us. We're the ones who ooze into entrepreneurship. When someone asks me how long I've been in business, I stall. I have a hard time pinning down the exact date. I want to explain that it's a long road, the same way couples who have lived together a long time before they got married always add the cohabiting years to the married years.

Officially, I got my sales and use license in 1980. That's when I started to pay taxes and declare myself a business rather than the hobby label the government applies to people who don't make much money at what they do. But I'd kinda, sorta, maybe considered myself to be in business before that date. I had shown and sold my work at a craft show, conducted a workshop or two, taught adult education courses. These were the foundation of my business, what it eventually would become.

But I don't tell people I started my business in 1973, because I didn't really feel like I was in business back then. Maybe I'm afraid that they'd expect more of me if they knew I'd been in business that long. Also, it didn't feel official—real—until I got the license and started sending in quarterly taxes.

Feeling as if I was running a "real" business came in stages. When I started to recognize and be recognized by other craft artists at shows, I began to feel like an entrepreneur, and I registered for courses to learn more about entrepreneurship. When a newspaper published an article about my work, I felt like a professional. Getting national press made my small company seem more real. When I got my 800 number, I decided that now I was really in business. When I incorporated in 1993, I thought: it's official now. It was a number of stages, small, incremental steps. My business incubated for years before it could withstand the rigors of the commercial world.

Would I do it differently today? Yes, if I were starting a new business. The slow way my business grew was exactly right at each stage of my life. When I had young children, the business was small. Now that my children are grown, the business is big, and I'm free to fly all over the world, and I do.

※　※　※

LESSON 5
What makes you unique makes you successful.

When I tell people that Arnold Schwarzenegger is my role model, they look at me as though I'm crazy. But Arnold's message continues to resonate for me. In an interview on TV with Barbara Walters, he said that when he came to this country he was repeatedly given three pieces of advice. He was told that no one in this country was interested in bodybuilding, that he had to lose his accent because no one would be able to understand him, and that he had to change his name, because how on earth was anyone going to remember Arnold Schwarzenegger?

Making my living as an egg decorator was not an easy path, but like Arnold Schwarzenegger, what makes me hard to comprehend, unique, and memorable is exactly what has made me successful.

※   ※   ※

LESSON 6

Truly understanding your core values will make some choices easier to refuse.

"Save your red lights." I remember the advice I heard at a parenting group many years ago. "If you say no to too many things, your children won't recognize when your 'no' really means something. You only get so many red lights." I decided that my red lights would be used to prevent poor grades, substance abuse, and teen pregnancy. Eating too many Halloween treats and staying up past bedtime playing video games were not going to be issues I badgered my kids about.

Similarly, defining what is and is not OK for my entrepreneurial life has helped me recognize my core values:

- Having time for the people I care about.
- Feeling valued for what I do.
- Keeping my life uncomplicated.

So I flashed red lights at opportunities that would interfere with those choices. When my children were young, I did not participate in activities that required a lot of travel. I simply did not put myself into arenas that would prevent me from taking care of my children.

One October, after my children were grown, I received a phone inquiry that tested my values. A high-ranking executive had received one of my custom-designed eggs as a present from a client. She was so delighted she wanted to hire me to create a gift for each of the corporation's key employees.

My cranial cash register began feverishly calculating the possibilities. I thought it would be not only workable but also profitable to fit one or two dozen extra $300 pieces into my production schedule. "About how many gifts would that be?" I inquired. "We'd need a thousand," she replied. "And our budget would allow for $30 to $35 per gift." A $35,000 budget! How could I help this woman? I asked her for twenty-four hours to consider her offer.

In that price range, I would be able to provide my lowest-cost items, holiday ornaments. To make them unique to the receivers, I would add the company logo to the design and personalize each one with the employee's name.

I began mentally lining up other egg decorators I knew and determined the cost of subcontracting. I calculated the time it would take to negotiate with each one. I considered the systems I'd need to develop for purchasing plus packing and shipping such an enormous order. I visualized this executive's thousand employees opening their gifts and what their reactions would be. I didn't like what I saw. My art form requires a unique audience. Not everyone loves what I do, or appreciates the heart and soul that go into the making of each piece. I know that good whiskey takes years to reach perfection, but I wouldn't appreciate receiving it as a gift even if it had my name written on it. My visualization captured the picture of several confused recipients dangling their ornaments quizzically and saying, "An egg?"

All three of my core values—having time, keeping it simple, and feeling valued—would be challenged by this opportunity. Since my bottom line is not measured in dollars, I said no to the executive.

※　※　※

LESSON 7

It is possible to continue doing the work you love for as long as you like.

It was an opportunity I couldn't refuse. I got a call from a producer at *The Carol Duvall Show* asking if a crew could come and do a story on me—a field show, they called it. Craft artists are videotaped in their studios discussing and demonstrating what they do. Show representatives asked if I would follow it up with a visit to their television studio in Burbank, California. Multiple appearances on national television sounded like a very good idea until I started making the arrangements.

To make the airplane trip affordable, my publisher, who was paying my fare, asked that I spend a Saturday night in Burbank to save some money. Because my brother and his family live in Los Angeles, I knew I could stay with him, and I agreed. Also, I realized it was an opportunity to combine business with pleasure. However, I knew I would lose five working days by going. Would it be worth it?

WIIFM—the abbreviation for "what's in it for me"—is a question business owners are constantly asking when opportunities arise. Although the allure of being on national television is thrilling, using precious workdays can be questionable. Net-net, what was the benefit to this artist? The answer to that was simple: Carol Duvall.

Having a role model like Carol Duvall is an inspiration. She's twenty years my senior and still going strong. She's feisty, smart, and down-to-earth. Until a few years ago, her excellent crew, who was devoted to her, helped her reach millions of Americans twice daily on HGTV. Though no longer appearing on that network, Carol is still active and admired in the craft industry. I met Carol in the early 1990s in Phillipsburg, New Jersey, at the twentieth anniversary of a craft show called the Eggsibit. At the time, Carol was with *The Home Show*, a network program starring Gary Collins that included her five-minute craft portion. She was cruising the Eggsibit with her camera crew recording footage of the event. They stopped by my display for an interview, recording my work, among others', for future TV audiences to see. I was immediately attracted to Carol with her bright red eyeglasses and her no-nonsense approach. So, as she and the camera crew finished taping at my booth, I asked her if she would be available for dinner. When the other artists saw us leave the hall together later that day, they probably wondered how I got so lucky. I simply asked her. Just asking for what I want is one key to my success as an entrepreneur.

Before I flew to California, I asked the producer if she could arrange a dinner for Carol and me. Fortunately, Carol's schedule permitted her to leave the set at a reasonable hour, and we had a wonderful time catching up on each other's careers. We also discussed how she might use my services in the future. I ended up with an opportunity to provide a paid, hands-on experience for Carol's entire staff and their families. That workshop was videotaped and aired as well.

The major economic benefit to spending all that time traveling and taping was the boost in sales that it gave my first book, *Decorating Eggs*. An even greater benefit was getting to work with someone like Carol, to observe her in her milieu, and to have her become an advocate for my business.

※　※　※

CHAPTER 2
Take the Plunge –
When Risks Pay Off

I had no idea what I was doing when I paid the $25 booth fee for an exhibit at the Pink Tent Festival in Stamford, Connecticut, back in 1973. It was my first investment in what became a thirty-year career in the craft industry.

Years later, preparing to enter the world of textile design while still engaged in my art business, I interviewed the surface design department chair at the Fashion Institute of Technology. Then I enrolled in several courses to learn the ropes. I quickly discovered that this field was not for me.

I started my coaching career without taking any courses, just hanging up a shingle when the opportunity arose. After two years of growing that part of my business, I signed up for classes to truly learn what a coach does. Then I enrolled in a program to become certified in the field.

The common thread here is taking action. Diving in is essential, whether it's getting your big toe wet or jumping off the ten-meter platform.

LESSON 8

You have to step out of your comfort zone, take risks, and survive the moments of dread to grow your business.

On Dr. Julie White's audiotape *Image and Self-Projection for Today's Professional Woman*, she relates a story about a friend in real estate. He made a killing on a property he had bought for a song and sold for a lot of money. His friends admired him for his expertise. However, he knew better. He confided to Julie that he had lost a lot of money on several other investments, and concluded, "If lucky breaks came labeled 'lucky break,' all of us would be rich." When friends and acquaintances think I'm lucky when some publicity hits, they don't know about the dozens and dozens of difficult investments of time and energy that didn't pay off at all. Those little miracles don't just happen. They happened because I did the work.

※　※　※

LESSON 9
In changing what is into what can be, we learn what we need to know.

Entrepreneurship is not easy. I have endured near-empty bank accounts, rejections, humiliation, envy, and despair. I don't like to talk about any of that. However, I find myself devouring any morsel of information written about someone else's bad experiences. I want a thorough description of how those people moved out of the dumps and moved on with their lives.

Hazelle Goodman, an actress, was quoted in the *New York Times* as saying, "There's no way to say it so it doesn't sound clichéd and preachy, but you've really got to hold on to what you believe. And keep breathing, crying, getting up, and going. Breathing, crying, getting up, and going. And then, you get there." She talked about how often she wanted to quit, to leave the movie industry, especially when a prospective manager said she was talented but too dark-skinned to work on camera. When I read that article, something inside me knew I, too, could endure—all I had to do was just keep going.

Through every painful experience, I learned something about how to conduct my business and my life. In my early craft-show days, I would watch enviously as the artist across the aisle was comfortable working the crowds who bought her exquisite handmade jewelry. She greeted several customers with hugs and big smiles as though she'd known them for years. She was full of enthusiasm, wrote orders continuously, and had a stunning display to boot. I grumpily acknowledged that I should try to start conversations with the people who were checking out my booth, and I started thinking about ways to make it more welcoming. And slowly, over the years, I redesigned my booth. I also studied assertiveness training and took seminars and weeklong workshops in personal development, and my ease with customers increased. My products improved, too. By the end of my exhibiting days, I had stopped noticing what was going on across the aisle, because I was too busy—I was enjoying the success I had formerly envied.

The geisha in Arthur Golden's *Memoirs of a Geisha* put it beautifully: "I don't think any of us can speak frankly about pain until we are no longer enduring it." When I give a keynote speech now, I tell humorous stories about those early days, about my embarrassment when I stood alone in my booth for hours on end, and the audience members laugh with me. They know I can speak about those painful times because I have created the results I used to envy. After the pain and suffering, learning, maturity, and eventually wisdom do come. But the light at the end of the tunnel may be too hard to recognize when we're suffering in the darkness of the tunnel. There doesn't seem to be a kinder, gentler way to get to the end of the tunnel and see the light.

※　※　※

LESSON 10
Plowing through the nitty-gritty details to complete each task creates big results.

One day while browsing through the self-development section at Barnes and Noble, I bumped into a friend. She asked me what I was looking for. I said I was researching the competition for a book I was thinking of writing. "Wow!" she exclaimed. "I always get a lot of great ideas, but they seem to fizzle after a couple of days. In fact, right now I'm thinking about opening a wellness center. It will have yoga classes, feng shui seminars, and a fountain two stories high in the center atrium. I can see it now." She was beaming, pleased with her dream.

"That sounds fantastic," I said, visualizing my own concept of her wellness center. "Where are you on the development right now?" "Oh, just imagining what it would be like." "Do you have a plan?" I asked. That seemed to be a difficult question for her. She looked at me, found an interesting title on the bookshelf in front of us, and the conversation was over.

Having a plan in any complex venture is essential, but breaking that plan into manageable, bite-size pieces is the key to success. One of the best methods for getting where you want to go is "single-handling," a term I first heard when I listened to Brian Tracy's tape *The Psychology of Achievement*. It is simply the ability to stay with one task from the beginning to its completion. Easier said than done.

"Billiard-ball brain" was the way playwright E. Katherine Kerr once described her method of attacking a tough job. That was how I operated. Let me describe a typical hour.

I need to send out an order to a customer. I go to the computer to print out the mailing label. While I'm there, I can't resist checking my e-mail. I see one from my friend Janet asking if our lunch date next week can be changed from noon until one. I switch screens to my calendar page to confirm the date and notice that I have an early afternoon doctor's appointment. I look up the doctor's office number and call to find out if I can reschedule it for a later time. His receptionist agrees, and when I go to enter that new appointment on my calendar, I hear my timer buzzing, indicating that an egg I put into the dye fifteen minutes ago is ready to be taken out. I move over to my design area and remove the egg, pleased that the color saturation is just perfect. Now, where was I?

The order I started to work on wasn't processed, and I had completely lost my momentum. This scenario has been played out repeatedly in a thousand ways in my life. One of the hardest things for me is to stay with a task from its inception to its completion. I get bored, frustrated, depressed, anxious, and ultimately lose my motivation. I want a distraction, a high, a reward. "This isn't as good as I thought it would be" and "I can't stay on hold waiting for this character to take my call" are typical things I say to myself.

Now, to get through these difficult periods—when I see that the job is going to take longer and will be more annoying than I anticipated—I take a deep breath or two, acknowledge to myself that I am single-handling this task (and aren't I great), and move forward. The high comes at the end when I actually complete the task. No matter how mundane it is, I feel good when I finish it. Then I can move on to the next item. The big goal, the wellness center of my plans, comes into clearer focus.

※ ※ ※

LESSON 11
Look before you leap to conclusions.

After completing the manuscript for my first book, I was invited to North Carolina to work with the publisher and the photography staff. Step-by-step photographs of the wax-resist process required my presence. Plus, they wanted my input for other layouts.

I overbuilt my importance as a writer. I fantasized a red carpet being rolled out for my arrival à la Jackie Collins. Failing that, I was hoping for a chauffeur-held placard reading: AUTHOR. In fact, my editor, who was to meet my flight, was unexpectedly detained. I had to call upon every ounce of maturity not to whine when she arrived. I had worked too hard on myself to carry on as I once had. I no longer held the belief that the world owed me. So the fact that the hotel didn't provide mints on the pillow before I went to bed was going to be OK with me.

Part of me had enjoyed playing the victim. Look what they've done to me again. Sigh. Long extended sigh. I used to love that role until I heard the expression "Once a victim, twice a volunteer." What? Take responsibility for what makes me unhappy? Unheard of! At one time in my career, until I was assured that a situation was perfect, I got my kicks out of finding fault, feeling mistreated. I was good at it, too. I could find lint on any collar. I might not have let you know, but I did keep a score card.

When I arrived at the photographer's studio in North Carolina, I had already worked with a number of photographers and art directors, each of whom had his or her own style. But, notwithstanding their differences, they all paid extreme attention to detail. I have stood by for what felt like hours while the perfectionist removed a mote of dust, endlessly repositioned a prop, or adjusted the light settings for the tenth time. The number of elements to be carefully considered when taking a picture seems endless.

My editor and I artfully composed my egg-decorating tools and materials to be shot as the first chapter opener—a full-page image facing the text. It looked pretty good. We cautiously awaited the art director's arrival. I steeled myself for an hour of tinkering, test shots, and reworking of the layout. She arrived late, glanced at our layout through the lens of the camera, and said, "Looks good to me." I was dumbfounded that her cursory peek was sufficient for the quality I wanted in my book. Is that really the best angle? Shouldn't we be using a tripod? I didn't show my agitation because I was the guest, the author, but on the inside I seethed.

That night, when I went back to my mintless hotel room, I recognized that I needed to work on my attitude. I was suffering; they weren't. "God, grant me the serenity to accept the things I cannot change, the courage to change the things I can, and the wisdom to know the difference." I said the serenity prayer over and over and over again. I not only recited it, I also paid attention to the words I was saying. Either I was going to have the courage to open my mouth or I needed to accept what I could not change.

The next morning before we drove to the photography studio, the editor brought me to the publisher's headquarters. As we were waiting to say hello to various staffers, I ambled over to the library filled with the company's publications. I opened several to the credit page, checking my team of players. Each volume they had produced was magnificent. The layouts were elegant, the photographs rich and inviting.

Did my reciting a prayer affect the contents of those pages? Or did my change in attitude allow me to see my world differently? I realized that my bad attitude was a cover for my feelings of insecurity. I was afraid. I was in an unknown environment with people I'd just met, working on my life's work, my baby. My old behavior pattern had prejudiced my mind. In the end, my book was beautiful.

※   ※   ※

LESSON 12
Don't quit before the miracle.

At least once a year, I get ready to pack it all in, give up, shut the doors on my business, and get a job collecting tolls on the highway. This usually happens after my phone gets quiet. Then I notice that my bank account is getting lower, and I find myself spinning my Rolodex to see what stone I have left unturned. Just as I am about to scan the classifieds, at the last moment I am saved. An opportunity I sought months before or a referral from a year earlier contacts me.

This roller coaster of emotions has been with me all my life. Most of my entrepreneurial friends tell me they go through something similar every year. It's a good thing we have one another—we can call each other up and say, "Don't quit before the miracle. You can count on it. The miracle always comes through. Allow the universe to manifest."

One summer when the world seemed to have gone on vacation and my monthly revenue was lagging, the phone rang. A lead I had followed up on months before to coach a leadership team resulted in the decision to move ahead immediately. I get prospects all the time who solicit my information but are not quite ready to begin the coaching process. The timing and extent of this opportunity were beyond my wildest dreams. The first month's fee for this assignment was exactly what I needed to earn for all of July. It was manna from heaven.

These painful stretches, when we're not sure how long we can endure, remind me of childbearing. Being an entrepreneur is occasionally like being pregnant. During my first pregnancy, the Lamaze instructor told us about the stages of delivery—labor, transition, birth. I had heard plenty about labor and birth but nothing about transition. "Transition," our instructor informed us, "is the hardest part of the process. It's painful and there is little time to rest between the contractions. Thankfully, it is also the briefest part, although it doesn't feel that way."

Transition is the stage when the labor room nurses get cursed at and mothers say, "I can't do this." Sounds a lot like what I go through when I can't see my next opportunity over the horizon. I want to quit, it's painful, and I'm angry. The advice to women in labor, other than doing pelvic tilts, also applies to anxious business owners: concentrate on relaxing, use visualization, and stay focused on the goal. In other words, have faith and carry on.

※   ※   ※

LESSON 13
When you get an inspiration, go for it.

"Do you think," Buddy asked me, "if I wrote a detailed letter to Clinton about the legendary Oh Hell games Matty, Kenny, and I used to play, he would join us for a round?" My husband had recently read an *Esquire* article about President Clinton and his passion for Buddy's favorite card game, a significant piece of my partner's youth. Now a retired English department chairman, Buddy would surely write a persuasive invitation.

I could easily imagine Bill Clinton getting a huge kick out of playing cards with Buddy and the guys. And now that Clinton had a home in nearby Chappaqua, New York, it would be workable. However, I wasn't sure if the letter would ever reach Clinton, and if it did, would he respond? But my husband was stymied—he wanted a guarantee before he made the effort.

Buddy's question made me realize that I used to be like Buddy. When I get an inspiration now like Buddy's, I run with it. Taking action moves me toward my wishes and dreams, and it strengthens the muscles I need for ultimate success.

I would have loved to have known in advance the answer to the question "Do you think that Neiman Marcus will be interested in co-producing my 'Dozen Eggs' project?" The only way to get an answer was to ask the buyer. I called her with my heart in my throat, and I found out that she wasn't interested. I wanted to hang up quickly, weep and wail, and throw the project away. Instead, I took a few deep breaths, called a good friend to whine and be comforted, then made a list of other potential buyers. Tiffany buyers also rejected the idea of co-producing but said they might be interested in future projects after seeing how this one turned out.

All this trying and failing made me refine my dream, my attitude, and my pitch. By the time I brought it to Artoria in New York City, it was packaged in a form that interested the company enough to partner with me.

"Go for it" has become my mantra when it comes to risk taking. Too many people look back on their lives and regret that they were afraid to take a risk to achieve a goal.

*   *   *

LESSON 14

Trust the instinct that moved you to write a task on your calendar, and follow through with it.

Did you ever get a great idea? It just comes to you and somehow you know that it's right. It goes on your to-do list. The day you appointed arrives, and you look at your list and say to yourself, "What could I possibly have been thinking? This will never work! I'll feel like a fool taking this step."

It has been my experience that if I second-guess inspiration, I lose. When I go with the initial, inspired feeling, even when I've lost the inclination, something wonderful happens. For example, I call customers ten days to two weeks after I mail off the artwork they've ordered. As soon as I finish packing a shipment, I go to my calendar and mark a date two weeks in the future to place that call.

An art professor of mine had ordered a decorated egg for his collection. I created it, shipped it, and made a note to place a follow-up call. When I saw his name pop up on my to-do list two weeks later, I had an inner dialogue that went like this: "If he really liked the egg, he would have called me. He must not have liked it. Uh-oh. Maybe I shouldn't even call. What if he didn't like my work?"

I called. His response was definitely worth it. "I've been meaning to call you. I love the egg! I'm sorry I didn't call. I'm as bad as my clients are. I hate it when they don't call me to tell me they like what I've done. I'd actually like to order a couple more."

＊ ＊ ＊

LESSON 15

As difficult as it is, you can teach yourself to believe you deserve what you charge for your work.

I thought I would throw up. I can still recall the feeling in my stomach when Beverly Ellsley, an internationally known interior designer, approached me at a craft fair in the early 1980s. She had just bought several dozen of my eggs at $35 apiece to give as gifts to magazine editors. As I was boxing them up, she said, "These should really go for $300 each."

It took me awhile to understand why I got sick when she said that. My internal voice was telling me, "You don't deserve that much money for your work. You're an impostor." However, another voice whispered, "She could be right, you know. This is quality work. This is art." But the impostor was insistent: "Who do you think you are, calling this art?" (This was years before I read *The Artist's Way*, which deals with the limiting beliefs many artists harbor.)

After more than two decades of practicing my art, marketing my work, and nursing my personal growth, I have come to grips with the impostor and slowly raised the selling price of my eggs from $8 apiece in 1973 to nearly $500 each in 2004 for the most ornate designs. In the early years, customers were surprised at the low prices and told me they were worth more. As I raised my prices, comments like this became rarer. I heard customers say, "They're worth it."

They are worth it also because their commercial value escalated as I gained recognition for my eggs in the marketplace. And I learned to appreciate my God-given talent to create these unique pieces. In return, I am willing to pay the price for a one-of-a-kind product another artist created, knowing full well that I can't walk into any department store in the country and find a comparable piece. I also acknowledge the persistence it took to keep plying my craft in the face of overwhelming odds against its success.

I no longer feel like an impostor for charging such prices for eggshells. I deserve it—professionally and emotionally. These prices are not arbitrary; they reflect the skill, uniqueness, and acceptance of my product.

At a recent networking event, a new acquaintance familiar with the corporate market suggested that I do seminars for corporate executives. "You could charge $10,000 for an afternoon session." Uh-oh. The same lesson in a new package.

※　※　※

LESSON 16
Step out of your comfort zone when someone asks you to do something that seems hard.

When I asked a new acquaintance what she did for a living, she said she was an interior designer. I was interested because I was redoing a bedroom in our house. I asked her several questions and wrote down some resources she recommended. As we were about to take our seats for the evening's program, she leaned over to me and whispered in confidence, "That's the first time I've ever said out loud that I'm a decorator. I've been taking courses for two years now, and it's what I really want to do." Up to that moment, I had fully accepted her for what she claimed to be. After the explanation, I began to question her recommendations.

In my early days attending networking events, I would never introduce myself to someone standing alone. Instead, I would sidle up to a friendly-looking cluster of women and hope that my interesting name tag—Jane Pollak, An Egg by Jane—would attract their attention. And it did. "An Egg by Jane?! What is that?" someone in the group would invariably ask, allowing me to enter the conversation. For years I worked on my response to that simple question as well as to others that came after it. A major benefit of joining a networking group is the opportunity to test your material in a comfortable environment.

After several years in the Entrepreneurial Woman's Network, I was asked to serve on the board of directors. Once you are on the board, it is assumed that you will take on any responsibility. At our May Grand Networking Event, I arrived early to set up the registration area. The president of EWN came over to me and said we were short on hostesses. Would I be willing to act as a greeter?

"What does that entail?" I stalled. "Just go up to everyone you see, introduce yourself, and start talking." It's that "just" word again. Like it's so easy. So I took a deep breath and acted as if it were the most natural thing in the world for me to do. An amazing thing happened. Everyone I approached bought me as the hostess with the mostest; I watched each woman's face brighten because of the attention I was paying her. She would open up and relax, relieved that she wouldn't have to spend the next hour examining her Filofax or rereading the program.

No one noticed I was way outside my comfort zone. The other women were too wrapped up in their own discomfort. I wanted to let them in on my secret that I had never done this before and was scared. But I refrained. What's the point? Just relish the success and move on.

Stepping out as a greeter, I had the opportunity to act like a hostess. The success I had at the job gave me the confidence to try that behavior again without the assignment. And I never confessed that I had to step out of my comfort zone to do it.

It works every time.

※　※　※

LESSON 17
To avoid feeling like an impostor, work through all the developmental stages first.

Ridgeway Elementary School in White Plains, New York, had two entrances for us children. Kindergartners through third-graders entered through the left-hand doors, fourth- through sixth-graders through the right. I still remember crossing over that invisible line one morning. I had something to tell my older sister, who was standing with her friends on the right side. "What are you doing over here?" she sneered at my invasion into her sacred space.

That didn't scar me for life, but after repeatedly invading her space, something she couldn't stand, I brought that worry about moving into a space where I didn't belong. It left me feeling that I had to earn the right to be anywhere. I know other kids hop right up to the plate, but I'll bet they're kids at the top of the pecking order—they were born first.

As a college freshman, I looked up to the seniors. I wondered how they got to be so mature, so all-knowing, so . . . old. When I became a senior by going through the same process all seniors go through, I couldn't fathom why those freshmen were looking up to me.

After several years of exhibiting my work, I felt I had earned the right to apply to Boston's Crafts at the Castle, the mecca of craft shows. After thorough preparation and hours of travel, I reached my destination, set up my booth, and walked around the exhibit hall to look for familiar faces. I saw only sixth-graders.

Eventually, the "big kids" worked their way around the show and took a look at my work, too. They admired my eggs and jewelry. Several offered to barter goods with me—the ultimate compliment. I felt accepted.

In *Ten Rules for Being Human*, by Cherie Carter-Scott, rule six says: "There" is no better a place than "here." When your "there" has become "here," you will simply obtain another "there" that will again look better than "here."

I now understand where my "here" and "there" are and what keeps me moving from one to the other. I acknowledge it as my process and go step by step or even skip a grade, depending on the situation.

※　※　※

LESSON 18
A coach can help the edgy transition of getting from here to there.

While learning new skills to coach teams and partnerships, I heard a term for the space between where you are and where you want to be: edge. Two examples in the coaching course manual are:

- Trying on a new idea or perspective.
- Being a shy person and choosing to speak up.

I recognize that feeling. It's where the word "edgy" comes in—that uncomfortable place between who you are now and who you'd like to become.

The illustration in that manual is an upside-down V with a curved arrow showing the arc of crossing from the old behavior or way of being to the new—from the shy person on the left of the V to the public speaker on the right side. The top of the V is the edge that needs to get crossed. Coaches not only recognize that the client is in a transitional phase, but also know how to gently (or occasionally forcefully) coax him or her over it to the desired outcome. Throughout my later career, coaches helped me cross edge after edge as I moved from being an artist to a speaker and then coach.

Over the holidays, I received a delightful card with a hand-drawn illustration by a young artist that more memorably represented "edge" than the one in my fancy notebook. The child had drawn a skier balancing precariously on the top of an upside-down V aka a youngster's interpretation of a mountain. The skier was on the verge of crossing an obvious edge: being on top of the mountain to taking the risk of descending it. Whether poised on top of a mountain or simply at an edge in one's life, coaching is a strategy that facilitates the process.

※　※　※

LESSON 19
Follow your urge and take action.

Where once I was frozen by indecision, being an entrepreneur for several decades strengthened my resolve to steer my own ship. Sometimes all those choices can feel overwhelming, particularly when you're determined to get things just right.

When should I make that phone call? Should I show my samples over lunch or by appointment? How many follow-up calls do I make? These are important decisions, but too much time spent thinking about them leaves too little time for acting on them. I prefer the take-the-plunge approach that releases the stress of perfection and moves things forward.

An opportunity to take the plunge came when I was featured, along with two other entrepreneurs, in a cover story for *Westport Magazine*. It was a coveted moment in the spotlight that I was thrilled to be a part of.

When the magazine hit the newsstands, I felt an urge to reach out and thank the people who had helped make it possible. Using my take-the-plunge mantra, I suggested to my co-cover girls that we express our gratitude in a more personal way. We created and mailed out invitations for a thank-you tea party, knowing that if we put it off the moment would pass and the opportunity to show our appreciation would be lost.

More often than not, it's fear of the unknown that keeps you in a three-to-get-ready mode. Not knowing exactly how things will turn out can be scary. But in the absence of a crystal ball, a leap of faith can be your best bet. Take that new idea and run-it-up-the-flagpole-to-see-if-anyone-salutes. Getting it out there puts you in the running for success. And, if you don't happen to get the results you'd hoped for, you'll still have gained vital information to guide you toward your next move.

We had the party, which showed our appreciation and surprised our benefactors—the writer, editor, photographer, makeup artist, and stylist—and created a lasting feeling of warmth.

※　※　※

LESSON 20
Measure your bottom line not just by dollars alone.

As each tax season arrives, at least one of my creative clients asks, "Should I be looking for a job?" One of my most gifted clients (I'll refer to her as Sue—not her name) and I had this discussion one early April day. Sue had just met with her accountant*, a quilting hobbyist, who gave Sue dire warnings about her financial future. I mention the hobby thing because I believe it has an impact here.

People who aren't pursuing their dreams, who haven't taken the risk to "live" their art, may not be the most reliable sources for creatives to listen to. I know I may get into trouble here, but I strongly advise my clients to manage their feedback, consider the source, and make their own decisions about which bottom line to regard. When you're happy in your life, with whatever work you choose to be doing, you're not as likely to step on someone else's dream.

Sue, by the way, had had her best year ever financially. She started our conversation by saying that the accountant "doesn't know my work," which spoke volumes from the get-go. Sue creates extraordinary, groundbreaking work in textiles. She'd been awarded two grants, curated shows in her area of expertise, and developed a collection of pieces for a museum exhibition. Sue is not in debt, has a newly renovated studio that has added value to her home, and has a business that is self-sustaining. Her family is supportive, loving, and proud. Considering the global economic downturn of 2008 and beyond, my value system says this represents immeasurable success. In addition, Sue's business paid for her to travel to museums and exhibits, for all of her materials, for the expenses of networking and socializing with peers, and for the many volumes she's read in her field and for inspiration.

In my book it comes down to values. When you're happy in your life, passionately pursuing the work you were put on this earth to do, giving off positive energy because you've got it to give, then your tax return is not the measurement to hang your hat on. Create your own personal accounting system for April 15 and on it measure your health, your joy in living, your mental attitude, your relationships, and your sense of connectedness in the world. Then decide whether you need to go look for a job.

By the way, at the end of our coaching call, Sue said, "I can't not be who I am." Sometimes these incidents show up in our lives to remind us how much what we do means to us.

Disclaimer: I love my accountant, Janis Siegel, CPA, who has never even hinted that I should look elsewhere for employment. This entry is not anti-accountants, only anti-dream killers in whatever guise they enter your lives.

※　※　※

CHAPTER 3

Smart (Yet Simple) Strategies

I described to a friend a situation I was having in one of my eyes. I had constructed in my lurid imagination that it was the first sign of a brain tumor or worse. He said, "Sounds like a floater." He assigned a name to that black mote that was repeatedly passing through my vision path. As soon as he named it, not only did my fear go away, but I also stopped noticing its presence.

Over the decades in my business, I've experienced the phenomenon of becoming aware of a strategy or tool for the first time and being transformed. Whether it was learning the SMART strategy for setting goals or being told that "trying" wasn't doing, each of these individually learned skills has accumulated into a wealth of experience, knowledge, and comfort with business ownership.

LESSON 21
Never apologize for organizing your day.

A friend of mine had two daughters who attended a respected private school in Boston. Like many mothers, she took an active role in their education and became an involved parent. As her daughters grew, so did her interest in the school, and she eventually became a dean there. At a function in that city, I was chatting with a group of women. One of them had children at my friend's school, so I asked her casually if she knew Nancy. She rolled her eyes and said, "Now there's a woman with an agenda." The implication was clear: Nancy was an opportunist, and anything she achieved was wrought not by hard work but by womanly contrivance. Having an agenda—a plan—was not looked upon kindly.

One spring weekend when another friend's daughter was getting married out of town, I shared a hotel room with two women. We all woke up early the day of the wedding. I sat up in bed and said, "I have a plan. I'm going to do my meditation and then go for a walk. I want to have breakfast at the waffle house up the block afterward. Anyone want to join me?" I didn't get any takers, but I followed my plan anyway and thought nothing about it again. Later that day, one of my roommates took me aside and informed me that I had annoyed her. I thought she was overreacting but accepted her feelings and was glad she felt comfortable enough to voice them to me. Several months later, she brought it up again. "Remember how I told you that I didn't want to be told about your plan when we were in Baltimore? I realize now I was mostly annoyed because you had a plan . . . and I didn't."

Since I learned the tools and strategies for goal setting, I've had a plan for each day, each month, and each year of my life, and I've stopped apologizing for it.

※　※　※

LESSON 22
Attention to detail matters.

Describing how I selected eggs to decorate took several paragraphs in my first book. When I was explaining the differences between white eggs and brown eggs, I paused. I knew that I had heard something about their nutritional value but couldn't remember. I knew that I could craft a sentence that disguised my lack of knowledge: Some people think that brown eggs have greater nutritional value. Or: Brown eggs are often perceived to have greater nutritional value.

But sentence one made me feel like a fraud, and sentence two bored me. I became curious and wanted to find out the truth. Students had asked me the question before, but it wasn't a detail that concerned me. My thoughts turned to Anne Lamott. *Bird by Bird: Some Instructions on Writing and Life* is one of my all-time favorite books. Reading it made me want to be a better writer. I used to resent interrupting my writing to research a word or a thought, but Anne Lamott considered it an adventure.

For example, when she needed to find the exact word for that wire thing on top of a champagne cork, she called the Christian Brothers Winery. This is how she described the process: "I got a busy signal. I really did. So I sat there staring off into space. I watched the movie in my mind of the many times I'd passed those vineyards and remembered how, especially in the early fall, a vineyard is about as voluptuous a place as you can find on earth." She made the process interesting, and the research became a journey. The word for that wire thing, she eventually learned, is hood.

I loved how Anne Lamott respected and crafted each word. She gave time and energy to do the job. Attention to detail in decorating eggs was my job. Why not transfer that ability and dedication to whatever I was focusing on? I called the University of Connecticut—well-known for its agriculture department. A professor told me that the nutritional value is the same. I could now inform my students and my readers that there is no difference.

※　※　※

LESSON 23

When someone gives you a lead, do the necessary work, even though the rewards aren't known in advance.

Somewhere between curtailing my full-time egg-decorating business and receiving the contract to write my first book, I entertained the notion that I would like to become the next Laura Ashley. I put out the word to my colleagues and began introducing myself as a textile designer at networking events.

Qualified leads come in unusual packages. At one Entrepreneurial Woman's Network lunch, a fellow artist tapped me on the shoulder and signaled me to come over to where she was sitting. She told me, "I was at my parents' house in Sag Harbor over Thanksgiving and was talking to their neighbor who is an interior designer. When I told him about your work, he said he would like to meet you." Sag Harbor sounded like the boonies to me, but being a polite woman, I kept listening. I didn't know Sag Harbor was an upscale artistic community on the tip of Long Island—a favorite getaway for successful New Yorkers.

Today I would qualify that lead by checking Google.com, but this was several years before that technology existed. So I had to trust the relationship and begin the pursuit of her parents' neighbor. Although it was a warm lead, the designer did not immediately respond to my call. I usually try once, leave a message, wait a week, and try again. Additionally, I might send a postcard or note letting someone know that I'm trying to reach him or her. Then, I follow that with a third phone call a week or two later. If six varied attempts produce no response, I may go back to the person who gave me the lead, but I rarely pursue a lead more than six times.

The designer and I ultimately connected and arranged to meet at a restaurant he suggested in Midtown Manhattan. I was sitting at the bar when the owner of the restaurant approached me. I told him I was waiting for Charles Morris Mount. It turned out that he had designed this restaurant's magnificent interior. "Can I get you anything while you're waiting?" the owner asked. It seemed as if doors were opening already. I was grateful I hadn't given up after the second or third unreturned call. I prayed he would like my portfolio.

Charles Morris Mount arrived at the appointed hour and was gracious in assessing my work. He listened as I described my career development and my new goals in the field of textile design. He liked my work enough to give me a referral to a design house in Lower Manhattan that he used frequently. Its specialty was fabrics for institutions such as restaurants and hospitals.

I followed that lead to the president of the company. Again it took several attempts to connect, but the designer's name became the magic wand that got me a return call. The president passed me along to the head of design (more calls, more time), who booked an appointment with me. I brought in my portfolio for her assessment. Upon seeing my work, she understood how she could apply my talents, although there was still one more person to see—the woman who would ultimately provide me with assignments.

Following this lead took a lot of time, phone calls, and perseverance, but thousands of dollars of work would result from that tap on the shoulder at a networking lunch.

※　※　※

LESSON 24
Get comfortable asking about money.

Polite young men and women are not brought up to say, "Show me the money!" Learning to ask how much you're going to be paid or informing a prospect about your fee are grown-up steps on the way to becoming a successful entrepreneur. For me, asking for my fee has been an ongoing struggle that has become easier only with practice and success.

After months of pursuing a lead to provide textile-painting services, I finally met the woman at the design studio who would be using my work. I thought I was home free. She started me off with a paint-by-numbers assignment that she offered me $25 per hour to do. I love it when there's clarity, even if it's less money than I wanted. Telling me the rate of pay saved me the discomfort of potential rejection and pain. The painting went well and the assignments continued.

After a few months of working with this arrangement, my client offered me a design assignment that allowed me more creativity. I gladly accepted it. As I progressed with this freelance project, I began mentally calculating my time at the $25-per-hour rate. However, this time I was not just painting the design; I was also conceiving and adapting it to specifications. I estimated that the job would cost her $600 at the established rate. But I was feeling disgruntled, underpaid. This work required a higher level of skills than simply matching colors and filling them into an existing pattern.

She was pleased with my finished work, but I had not yet negotiated a new fee. I knew I had nothing to lose by asking the question when the subject of invoicing came up: "Shall I bill this project the same way as the others you've given me?" Notice that nowhere in that question was a request for higher compensation. For me, it was still a step forward. "No," she replied. "We pay $1,200 to $1,500 per design. What do you think it's worth?" Given the choice, I opted for the high end and received it.

Slowly, I have added the money question or statement to every business relationship I've entered. I simply say, "Can we discuss the financial arrangements?" or "What does your budget allow for breakout sessions?" or "My fee is . . . ." Sometimes the conversation that follows is pleasant. Sometimes it's difficult. But the best part is that when it's over I know exactly where I stand and so does the client. I don't suffer the agony of not knowing. My sense of self-worth is reinforced by knowing ahead of time what rate I will get for the level of work I am doing.

※　※　※

LESSON 25

When someone asks you how you got that incredible break, the simple answer is hard work.

One afternoon, a production crew that included a cameraman, sound guy, producer, and director plus two dot-comers spent six hours in my studio taping an interview for network television. That opportunity had the potential to result in the best exposure my small business had encountered so far. I was excited and told my walking partner about it the next day. When she asked me how it happened, in my mind I went through the many stages that led to it.

It all started this way: Nine years earlier during a routine dental checkup, my dentist's assistant and I chatted, and between rinses I described my work to her. She asked if I'd seen *Victoria*, a relatively new magazine that had a monthly feature about unusual business cards from all over the country, and suggested I send in my card. I trusted her instincts and promptly went to the nearest shop to check it out. The magazine was gorgeous, and the page Julie described was just right for my kind of business. I mailed in my card.

Victoria checked me out thoroughly. Editors contacted me for more information to ensure that I could handle the surge of orders that would follow such publicity. I had to assure them that I had support materials showing my products and prices. I also had to be interviewed by an editor at the magazine. It worked. My card and one of my intricately decorated eggs were featured in the April issue.

That May I met the editor in chief at an American Woman's Economic Development conference. She suggested that *Victoria* do a story on my work. More opportunities arose. My jewelry was featured in the magazine's circular; I participated in a chat room online with readers and spoke on a panel at a conference sponsored by the magazine. A few years later, Victoria chose seventy women, including me, to profile in a

book, *The Business of Bliss: How to Profit from Doing What You Love.*
And that's what prompted the television company to contact me.

Here's the true answer to the question "How did it happen?" I pursued a lead, followed up, showed up, stayed in touch, sought out future
opportunities, pursued those, and continued this pattern for nine years.

I told my walking partner, "Just lucky, I guess."

※　※　※

LESSON 26
Stay with the process.

I continually need to remind myself to stay with the process. The tool I used to draw on my eggs needed to be regularly filled with beeswax. I often resented stopping to fill the small well with chips of wax because I was enjoying the drawing so much.

When I forgot to refuel the tool, I began to notice that the wax lines I was laying on the eggs were getting just the slightest bit scratchy, or some small dirt particles were showing up in the lines. These were indications that the tool was running low on wax. It's like when I'm driving my car and the refueling light goes on. I never want to stop and fill up. I'd rather just keep going.

However, both have been vital to my progress and process. Once my drawing tool was refilled, I felt free and had a renewed sense of purpose. The minor break refreshed me. And I could now use the energy I had lost in checking that wax supply for the creative task at hand.

※　※　※

LESSON 27
Translate the success of someone you admire into realistic goals.

Shortly after college graduation, Lindsey, my oldest child, attended a goal-setting workshop I gave and was stumped by the assignment. She didn't know what direction she wanted to take in her life and told me, "I'm not sure how to make this a goal, but I know I'd like to be the next Anna Quindlen." Having someone you admire is a good yardstick in setting a goal. Lindsey needed to figure out what it was about Anna Quindlen that appealed to her, and then she had to work backward to determine what steps it would take to get there.

"What is it about Anna Quindlen that you admire?" I asked her.

"She wrote those great columns in the *New York Times*, and now she's a novelist. There are lots of journalists and writers out there."

"What particularly appeals to you about Anna Quindlen?"

"Her columns speak to me as a woman."

"What else?"

"I like that she's married and has kids."

"Anything else?"

"I'm impressed by her willingness to give up her job at the *Times* to be with her kids and write novels."

Working this way, Lindsey was able to extract a set of goals for herself. She could transform Anna Quindlen's attributes—working for the *Times*, appealing to a female audience, and having a family she's committed to—into small chunks in order to form long-term goals. Lindsey had to do the following:

- Find out how to write for the *New York Times*.
- Write and submit articles about her experiences as a college student.
- Continue dating as a precursor to choosing a husband and having a family.

It's smart to choose a role model you can adopt. Who wouldn't like to have the genius of Bill Gates, the leadership of Gloria Steinem, the culinary talents of Julia Child, the kindness and generosity of Mother Teresa, and the looks of Anne Hathaway or George Clooney? If we try to put together an unrealistic combination of talents, we defeat the possibility of ever measuring up.

By selecting Anna Quindlen, a real human being, Lindsey doesn't need to worry about her role model's fashion expertise or technological wizardry. She can focus on the elements that are important to her: family values and writing skills.

My role models continually change. In my early career in crafts, my model was Linda Carr, who brought her curly-haired daughter to work at craft shows and was sought as a designer by Vogue Patterns. Now my model and mentor is Oprah Winfrey, who continues to empower women while continually transforming herself.

✳   ✳   ✳

LESSON 28
Even when copycats threaten your livelihood, keep doing what you do best.

I couldn't believe my eyes. I was just about to ask, "Where's Linda?", when I finally found my friend's exhibit in the maze of colorful merchandise spread across the Guilford Green in Connecticut. On closer inspection, though, I realized it wasn't Linda Carr's booth at all. The dolls looked a lot like Linda's, but something was missing. They didn't touch me the way Linda's had.

Before I met her, I was struck by the display she had created for her work. I had attended my first Guilford Handcrafts Expo—the grand-daddy of craft shows—to see if becoming a craft artist was for me. Linda and I became friends a year later at the Westport Handcrafts Fair (my first craft show) when she offered to trade her dolls for my eggs.

In her Guilford booth, Linda's products hung from swings, sat on diminutive rocking chairs, or posed in other lifelike stances. The boy and girl dolls were dressed in Oshkosh overalls; the young maidens wore fine Italian-cotton print dresses. Their embroidered faces and hair made of yarn turned them into children you wanted to take home. Her competitor, at the booth I had mistakenly thought was hers, had displayed her dolls in the same poses as Linda's and copied their outfits, expressions, fabrics, and labels.

When I told Linda about the person who was imitating her dolls, I was impressed with how she handled the situation. Rather than kick and scream to the show management, as I might have done, she saved her energy. She invented new designs, spent quality time with her customers, and ignored her rival, who disappeared a year or two later.

Ironically, a few years later, a customer accused Linda of copying another person's designs. Linda told the misinformed patron with a gentle smile, "I'm not copying anyone. *I'm* the person who designs these dolls for *Vogue*."

※　※　※

LESSON 29

Time and turnover in your industry will provide opportunities to present the same idea more than once.

"Is that one of mine?" I asked the woman who was pointing to the pin on her blouse. It looked familiar, but I couldn't quite remember making it. She nodded and told me how much she enjoyed wearing it. I took a closer look. Often, I like my work better later than when I made it. I'm highly self-critical, so it's delightful to see one of my creations improved by time.

My friend Mary Ellroy, owner of the company GameBird, gave this phenomenon a name: "revisiting." She is an inventor who shares her project ideas and prototypes with the members of our mastermind group. Major toy companies have rejected her seemingly brilliant concepts only to be charmed by them a year or two later.

Mary has learned that there are always opportunities to revisit past inventions, assess them once more, and then demonstrate them to a fresh audience. Happily, sales often result. You could call her persistent because she doesn't take no for an answer, but the term "revisiting" has a nicer ring. It's casting a fresh look at work you've done, dusting it off, and exposing it to the light of day once more.

※   ※   ※

LESSON 30

Once you're on your own, the only person responsible for your life and well-being is you.

It's fun to make a bold move every once in a while. I took one in 1995 after I heard Kate White speak at an American Woman's Economic Development Corporation conference. At the time, she was editor in chief of *Redbook*. Her talk that afternoon was about gutsy versus good girls. Her message was funny and touching because the audience could relate to it easily. I wanted the women in my local networking organization to meet and hear Kate as well. Inspired by her message, I approached her after her talk and invited her to address my networking organization in Connecticut. She agreed.

Hearing her message a second time made me even more willing to take risks. Earlier that week, my publisher had sent me a mock-up of the front cover of my first book. It was ghastly. It looked like the cover of a religious textbook, not like a coffee-table book. I felt sick to my stomach when I thought about having to promote my work in that wrapper. Kate's talk revved my spirits, and I went out of my comfort zone, the one that would tell me it didn't matter. I called my publisher that afternoon, and he must have heard me because the cover was changed. When people ask how I got a particular article about me in the press or a seat at the head table, more often than not the answer is: I asked.

If we are fortunate when we are children, someone will keep an eye on us and encourage us to take advantage of opportunities that are appropriate. Once I was grown, I wondered who would say, "Jane, you really ought to meet that editor . . . send out a press release . . . see if anyone in your alumnae group can help you out." But once you're on your own, the only person responsible for that kind of encouragement is you.

※　※　※

LESSON 31
Set aside childhood behaviors that impede your success.

Forty-five women sat on the floor of an exercise studio, mirrors all around. One by one they shared intimate details of their lives, and it became clear that each had used relationships to fill a gaping hole inside them. Although I didn't share anything with them for several months, I recognized that this was a place I would feel comfortable. It marked the beginning of a transformation that affected my career, personal growth, and success.

For the first time, I began to address issues that had held me back in my life and, ultimately, in my work. I am not a psychologist and do not pretend that I am an expert in addictive behavior. But I am an entrepreneur who understands the enormous impact of personal dysfunction in a business. I have become part of a fellowship that offers practical, spiritual-based tools for managing my life. By using these tools daily, I have been able to set aside behaviors that impeded my success. I transformed myself from a shy young woman hiding behind an artistic gift to a mature adult who is willing to take her place in the world based on her talents, intelligence, and drive.

Eliminating my addictive behaviors helped me uncover the motivation behind most of my actions. When I become keenly and often uncomfortably aware of why I am behaving a certain way, I am more likely to change that behavior and do the right thing. When I was in an addictive mode, I would use a substance (sugar), a person (a phone call), or an action (procrastinating) to alleviate any discomfort a situation created. Today I no longer medicate feelings. I experience the pain and analyze why I'm feeling it. Then I move swiftly and directly to deal with its cause.

For instance, I never used to question a rejection or investigate why it happened. I simply figured I wasn't good enough. Now when I get a rejection, I take a moment to breathe and reflect on what I can learn from it. With the support of a coach, I will request five minutes from the decision maker to inquire what I might do to increase my chances in the future, what criteria I didn't meet, or whether anything else may have factored into the rejection. The response always teaches me something. Most important, however, is that I am no longer afraid to address an authority figure—a fear that held me back for too many years.

My personal transformation had a significant effect on the lives of four other people as well, the four people most important to me—my husband and children. Several years ago, when Lindsey, Robert, and Laura were all living at home, we had five different sets of needs. I called a family meeting and asked everyone to bring datebooks or calendars. We sat in our living room and discussed our upcoming events for the next month. The goal was to be supportive of one another and to make sure we knew who needed which car. When I described this forum to my counselor, he said, "Do you know what we call that?" I was sure he was going to say "anal," but his answer surprised and delighted me: "Functional." I couldn't have asked for higher praise.

※　※　※

LESSON 32
Trust your gut.

I visit Bergdorf Goodman, one of the most sophisticated and expensive department stores in the world, the same way I go into the Metropolitan Museum of Art. Both places display top-quality objects that are wonderful to look at and, in many cases, of incalculable cost. I go to gaze, to study great design and craftsmanship, and to be inspired.

On one trip I got more than I'd bargained for. As I was taking in a showcase filled with ornate jeweled boxes, my eye became riveted to one particular design. It was an enlarged metal and rhinestone reproduction of one of my original intricate egg designs. A dead ringer. I got the same feeling I used to get as a child when I discovered that my sister had worn my favorite blouse to school without asking permission.

I wanted to dismiss the feeling of being robbed of something that belonged to me. Instead, I wanted to feel flattered that a well-known designer was copying me. But I couldn't get past the fact that she had copied my art without permission or payment. My gut was telling me, "Don't ignore this." But I ignored my gut because I was afraid of whatever I needed to do to set this right.

Two days later, a friend from the Entrepreneurial Woman's Network called. She was an image consultant and personal shopper who spent hours combing Manhattan stores. "Jane," she said, "I was in Saks Fifth Avenue yesterday and saw your designs on some boxes there. I recognized them right away. Has someone licensed your egg designs?"

My feelings were reaching epidemic proportions. A third sighting at Bloomingdale's confirmed that I had to take action even though I didn't want to. I had never hired a lawyer and had no idea what my rights were, nor did I know how to proceed. Fortunately, at an EWN event the same month, I cornered an attorney and asked her for advice. She represented several creative clients and was familiar with such issues, so I hired her to handle the case.

Her first letter to the offending company was met with its complete denial of any wrongdoing. My lawyer's second letter was stronger, warning that we would bring evidence of the infringement to the stores' attention. The designer settled promptly, removed the copied pieces from the department stores, and paid my legal fees.

I received two lessons from that experience. The first one was immediate—the pleasure of seeing justice prevail. The second I learned years later: I could have handled the situation differently. I could have approached the designer and asked for recognition and payment. I could have formed an alliance with her. I think of how much I would have enjoyed owning a jeweled version of my eggs.

※　※　※

LESSON 33
Action is progress.

One of my coaching clients had a goal to write ten pages of her novel. She gave the following report: "I wrote quite a bit but can't remember whether I said the ten pages needed to be single- or double-spaced." There were chuckles of recognition in the mastermind meeting where she made her announcement. Someone teased her about what font size she used. Another asked her how wide the margins were.

The next person to share her success noted that she'd been "adjusting the margins" around her goal, too. Using the metaphor of "editing" goals became an amusing theme throughout the meeting.

What occurred to me during all of this talk was the knowledge that success is not measured in page numbers or margin widths. The measure of success is in the actions taken.

A wise mother offered me a parenting tip many years ago. She said, "As long as the general direction is forward, you'll be fine." That's sage advice in goal setting as well. If it moves you closer to your goal, that's success.

Mark Victor Hansen, the co-author of the *Chicken Soup for the Soul* series, once said his goal was to sell one million copies of the book in its first year of publication. He went into great detail about all the activities he had engaged in in pursuit of that goal. "We only sold 800,000. Was that a failure?" No, it was significant progress. Deadlines can be pushed ahead, but measurable actions are the stuff success is made of.

※　※　※

LESSON 34
Just start!

I first heard the term "sloppy copy" from a coaching group participant, designer Patricia Frank Sher. Her son Sam had learned the technique at school. It's simple, he explained. If you're stuck getting started, you just begin the work, and it doesn't have to be perfect.

Patricia loved the simplicity of the solution Sam's second-grade teacher had taught him. Stalled on the daunting task of starting her own project, a book about creating Jewish heirlooms, she embraced sloppy copy and got writing.

So often we're paralyzed by the belief that we need to have everything perfectly laid out before we can get started. Giving yourself permission to begin a project where you're most comfortable can get you out of the fear place and into action. I wrote the chapter on creating two-color eggs before I crafted the first chapter of *Decorating Eggs* because it came easily to me and got me started. The last piece of the writing project I tackled was actually that first chapter because it felt so daunting.

Another great way to free yourself when paralyzed by self-expectation is a similar practice called a "sober quota" (as mentioned in Julia Cameron's book *Finding Water: The Art of Perseverance*). A sober quota is about taking on a manageable amount of work to tackle.

Alcoholics Anonymous members talk about one day at a time, or one hour, or even one minute. It's an adaptable idea that can work for every challenge. I know that daily social networking is in my future, but this week all I need to do is spend one hour scrolling through my Facebook news feed.

Once again, action is the formula for success. After resisting blogging for at least a year, I set a goal of contacting an expert in the field who could help me get started. Then I scheduled my first phone training session with her. A week later, I sloppily wrote my first blog copy. By breaking down the overwhelming process of blogging into small measures of time and so-so efforts at first, I filled my sober quota and have been happily and less sloppily blogging ever since.

※　※　※

LESSON 35
Keep the focus on your own business development, not others'.

The Internet is a blessing and a curse for business owners. The good news is you can discover how unique your business idea or product offering is. The bad news is you can also find out how not unique it is. The better news is it really doesn't matter. There is room for everyone—if you take action.

One of my clients had an appealing and humanitarian concept for an online business involving products as well as community building. After spending hours online, she discovered many look-alike companies. In her words, "I freaked out!" Wisely, she shared her feelings with supportive peers who consoled and counseled her. "It's called 'competition' and you can handle it," they advised.

Another colleague told me how many hours she had been spending researching her business ideas on the Web. She was thorough and sincere and had accumulated mountains of knowledge about her industry. She studied the market up, down, and sideways. She knows her competitive advantage and her target audience. But her income had stalled. I gave her one word of advice: "Act!"

What both of these small-business owners experienced is analysis paralysis—the frozen state of inaction that comes from information overload. When this is your diagnosis, here's what I prescribe: Get crystal clear about what you need to know. For example, when selecting a printer for a project, I developed a list of specifications I was checking for. I limited the search to ten companies for comparison. I allowed myself one hour a day for three days (or a similar formula) to accumulate the data. I knew that once I received information from these printers, I'd have a good enough idea of the market. I committed to taking action by a specific date and enlisted a goal buddy to hold me accountable. Get clear, figure out how many or how much by when, and take action. Voila—you're out of paralysis and moving forward.

❊   ❊   ❊

LESSON 36
Eliminate minimizing words.

I instituted a 25-cent fine at my monthly Arts Forum meetings when they began. During these sessions, successful women artists shared successes, challenges, and goals with one another. Three signs sat discreetly but prominently in the middle of the group. Each displayed a word with the international "no" sign across it. They were "try," "just," and "little." Every usage incurred a penalty, which members anted up with less and less frequency as the year progressed.

In spite of the talent level, maturity, and sophistication of these fabulous women, those words often slipped into their statements and diminished the power of their messages. Only a few dollars were collected before everyone grew more conscious and sparing in their use of these minimizing words.

My own consciousness was raised many years ago when I heard Dr. Julie White, a professional speaker, on an audio series devoted to self-empowerment for women. She delivered a memorable lesson. After she had given a keynote address to a large audience, a gentleman came up to her and said, "I really liked that little speech of yours." Julie looked him squarely in the eye and said, "Oh, thank you. That was actually my jumbo speech."

I hear minimizers slipping frequently into conversation with business owners, both men and women: "Here's my little brochure." "That's just my rough draft of a book proposal." "I'll try to be there." When they're spoken in succession, it becomes clear how they diminish the effort involved or the accomplishment. As much as your visual materials make statements about you and shape your prospects' perceptions, your words have an enormous impact as well, not only on others but on yourself, too.

Edit your conversation and your correspondence with a fine-toothed comb. When writing, for instance, I make liberal use of the backspace key and consciously choose to make my language more powerful. For those of you who can remember the old days of typewriters and Wite-Out, we can thank our lucky stars for the joys of word processing.

As you become more conscious of noticing each "just," "try," and "little" you speak, catch yourself and restate your message using commanding language. The simple truth is most powerful of all.

Then give yourself a jumbo pat on the back.

※　※　※

LESSON 37
It takes brains and time to execute even the easiest of ideas.

If I had a nickel for every time I heard someone say, "That's a no-brainer," in reference to an undertaking that sounds easy . . . well, I'd have several dollars by now. The implication is that it's money in the bank and all you have to do is wave your magic wand and collect. Not so!

There was the "no-brainer" to republish my *How I Got on the Today Show* CD, taking it from loving-hands-at-home quality to first-rate professional product. That "no-brainer" required six long weeks of my time and attention.

Then there was the snap-of-the-fingers suggestion my colleague/client decided to try out. She's a professional organizer and knew it would be a no-brainer to open a store and sell products to her customers. I assigned her to a day shadowing a store owner for the retail experience. She didn't make it through the eight-hour shift. She was bored to tears and miserable staying in one location and not having the variety of experiences her organizing business offered. She bagged the idea posthaste. Thank goodness she hadn't committed to a lease before testing the waters.

The reality is that no-brainers and good ideas are a dime a dozen. The implementation is the unsexy, nitty-gritty hard work that takes time. When you get a great idea or no-brainer, create a mind map, jotting down what's entailed. What resources do you need? Whose services are required? What market will you reach and how?

Brains or no brains, following through on any agenda item requires much thought, considerable muscle, plenty of heart and soul, and dedicated time on the calendar. No-brainers? There are none.

※　※　※

CHAPTER 4
Always Be Marketing

I'll never forget hearing Tom Peters say in an audio lecture that if the pull-down tray of your airline seat is coffee-stained, the perception is that the plane's engine may not be clean either. That is going to impact your feelings about the airlines—to fly or not to fly with them in the future. Also note that no detail is too small. Everything counts. Even a coffee stain.

From the outbound message of our phones to the rapidity of our response rate to requests, we business owners are judged on all of it, not just our products or services. You are creating your brand experience with the clothes you wear as well as your handshake at a networking event.

Scary? Yes! But also a challenge and opportunity to express your uniqueness, memorability, and personal style.

LESSON 38
Take care of your image, and you will be taken seriously.

Throughout my career, I have been confronted with something common to legions of women who own their own businesses—not being taken seriously. For example, back in the mid-1970s, I taught my first adult education course. At a faculty gathering before the semester started, I was seated next to a man who asked what I was going to teach. He was offering a course in financial planning. When I told him I was going to teach quilting, he looked at me quizzically and asked, "Is there a book in that?" He doubted that there was enough content in the subject for a semester's worth of classes. My first thought was how little he knew. Then it occurred to me that he, like many other people, didn't know that quilting was an old American art form that had become popular again. Finally I realized that I was unhappy because he put me down and dismissed the value I was offering. The pain of his comment took awhile to register.

Another time, a salesman stopped by my home office to deliver an order. He looked around and remarked, "Oh, you really *are* a business." Because my office was in my house, he had predetermined I was not really a businessperson. A phone technician once spent hours doing the wiring for the dedicated business and fax lines in my renovated studio. While he attended to his job, I applied wax and dye patterns to eggs for an upcoming event. I noticed him glancing at me every few minutes, wondering what I was doing. After I showed him the process of decorating eggs at different stages, he was puzzled: "Is that really your job?"

It took me years to feel comfortable explaining what I did. Most often when I said I was an artist and Ukrainian Easter eggs my medium, the response was patronizing. I did more than decorate eggs. Even when I put my wares out to sell—when even I didn't know it would turn into a career—I was conscious that the public really didn't accept the fact that anyone could make a business out of egg decorating.

I realized then that it would be up to me to establish the seriousness of my enterprise. My craft industry role model was my friend Linda Carr—a doll maker and best-selling designer for Vogue Patterns.

She knows how successful she's been, how gifted she is, and what beautiful work she produces. She's not worried about how she is perceived. She's not compelled to explain the breadth of her business. It is enough for people to appreciate the creativity she has brought to our world.

❊   ❊   ❊

LESSON 39
If you really want something, pursue it directly.

Jealousy has often fueled my entrepreneurial fires. I subscribed to an elegant periodical called *Ornament*, which highlights handmade clothing, jewelry, and other collectibles. A monthly page dedicated to one artist features photographs of the artist's work, as well as a personal statement. Typically, when I come across features like this, I think: How do you get that magazine's attention? How do you make that kind of great exposure happen? Do you need to show up at the right exhibits with an impressive booth and goods? Does the publisher or editor have to be a fan? For months I looked at that page and drooled over its contents, jealous of the artist's good fortune in being selected.

On a whim one day, I called to find out how to get published in that magazine. I was told that any artist could submit photographs and a statement for consideration. I put together my statement, sent along a few slides, and promptly received a phone call notifying me that my statement would run in a future issue.

I did an immediate turnaround as I often do—akin to Groucho Marx, who remarked that he didn't want to become a member of any club that would accept him. Once the magazine accepted me, I was not so impressed by the magazine. I recognize this attitude now as a self-protection device. If I lowered my opinion of the magazine, I wouldn't be so disappointed if I didn't get a positive response later when my work appeared there.

※　※　※

LESSON 40
Perception is everything. Keep your message clear and consistent.

If a package comes in a brown wrapper, its origins are questionable. If it's engraved, it's pricey. If it's pink or purple, it's for women. We as consumers are trained to make judgments about every image that passes across our radar screens. The billions of dollars spent on marketing and advertising have taught us to evaluate products and services in a nanosecond. With information bombarding us at record levels, getting an entrepreneur's message across is a marketing challenge. I've experienced this from both ends of the spectrum—as a business owner and as a buyer of goods and services.

When I began showing my work at craft fairs, I placed my intricately decorated eggs in whimsical settings—cradled in a bird's nest or grouped in a porcelain bowl accessorized with a sterling silver spoon. The display did catch the attention of the crowds walking by. The eggs could be touched, even though discreetly placed signs asked onlookers to refrain from handling the work.

One day, an elderly, bespectacled woman entered my booth, inspected my display, reached her hand into the nest, lifted up three of my prettiest designs, and took out a $1 bill. "I'll take these," she said. Something about the image I had created with my display must have suggested to her that my eggs were 35 cents each, not the $35 each noted on the sign I had so carefully placed beside the bird's nest.

I knew that I had to alter the perception of what I was selling. The nest idea had to go. I began to exhibit my eggs in glass showcases or under glass domes, thereby informing the public that they were Art. The presentation reinforces your customer's expectation of what you are selling. I was saying my eggs cost a lot and were worth the money.

Bulgari, one of the most expensive jewelry stores on Fifth Avenue in New York, changed its image in the opposite direction, by making its wares more accessible. Where once a guard buzzed shoppers into the

store, now there was a revolving door. Where once all shoppers had to
be guided to a private room by a salesclerk before they could inspect the
jewelry, now all they had to do was enter the store and look at the jewelry
that was visible in glass cases, and a clerk would walk over to wait on
them. Bulgari management had decided its store was too intimidating
for American customers.

※ ※ ※

LESSON 41
It's necessary to dress the part.

"Your haircut is too suburban," the image consultant informed me. She taught the final session in a semester-long course for women who owned their own businesses. It was a wise move on her part to save this session for last. We students had grown comfortable with one another and understood exactly what each person needed to communicate to her marketplace.

One by one, we took our turn in front of the class to learn how we might improve our visual message. The accountant who wanted to attract a more creative clientele was advised to trade in her conservative navy suit for more stylish dresses and statement jewelry. No more tiny stud earrings. Chunky clip-ons would complete her look. The computer consultant was advised to cut off her ponytail. It conveyed a negative message to corporate clients. When it was my turn, the instructor asked me what image I would like to convey. "Artistic, sophisticated, stylish," I responded. After assessing me, she recommended a New York hairstylist as well as an outlet for designer clothing.

Our class had a reunion six months after that final session. What a delight to witness the transformations! Our accountant not only looked more creative and well-accessorized, but also reported that her business was taking off by leaps and bounds with the clients she had hoped to attract. The computer consultant had changed her hairdo and was successfully working with a number of corporate customers. Everyone loved my asymmetrical haircut and chic new outfit. I, too, had begun to feel more like the contemporary craft artist I wanted to be. Image is not the solution to everything, but dressing the part to support your work is a step toward business success.

※ ※ ※

LESSON 42
If you are going to compete in business, your marketing materials need to project the statement that you are a serious player.

At one of my marketing seminars, a man asked what I thought about his flier. With some hesitation and tact, I told him that his flier looked as though he had printed it in his basement. He was proud to admit it: "I did do it in my basement—on my own copier." He had missed my point. It's important to project the image that you're serious about your business. Nobody wants to know that you printed your material in your basement. All it does is broadcast what league you're playing in.

I found I had to upgrade the look and feel of my marketing materials to enter a bigger league. I had an elegant logo created to reach a more sophisticated audience than I had previously targeted, but my written materials did not match that upscale look. I knew I needed help conveying something about me and my products that I was unable to articulate. Through a referral, I met Marci Levin, a gifted copywriter. She spent the first part of our first meeting asking me about my business and reviewing my work and marketing materials. She appreciated the delicacy of my handwork and the uniqueness of my business. As soon as she said she was going to create a romance around my eggs, I knew I was in the right hands. I could never have come up with the word, but when she said it, I knew exactly what she meant—and couldn't wait for her to take charge.

Marci created several marketing pieces for me, starting with an insert in my brochure titled "The Opulent Egg." She wrote about "the timeless paisleys, classic Egyptian motifs, exquisite Ukrainian patterns—the world of vivid color and intricate design that is AN EGG BY JANE." That's romance! I loved what she wrote, believed it to be true, but could never have produced those words myself. I was too inhibited. Hiring Marci was the beginning of allowing other creative people to describe, illustrate, and promote my work. Their expertise gave me a much bigger image than if I had continued promoting myself. I was able to take a back seat to their talents and allow them to shape an image that would capture a wider audience.

The bonus of hiring a great copywriter is twofold. The mental and emotional time it would have taken me to create my own marketing messages is now devoted to doing what I do best—practicing my craft. Whether it's creating opulent eggs or leading remarkable women to uncommon success, I'm focusing my energies on my gifts and letting others express theirs.

※   ※   ※

LESSON 43

Get as much mileage as you can from opportunities that arise, but keep it honest.

After ten years of operating my business in Connecticut, I heard about an organization called the Entrepreneurial Woman's Network. I was impressed when I found out its headquarters were in a high-priced commercial location on the gold coast of Fairfield County. I wanted to learn more about the association, so I got in the car one morning to check it out. But rather than the office complex I was anticipating, I saw only a small, New England-style building with a sign out front that read, "Mail Boxes Etc." Having never heard of this company—this was 1989, long before Mail Boxes Etc. had popped up on every block—I went inside to find out if EWN had moved. "Oh, no. They're right over there in Suite 646," explained the proprietor, pointing to a three-by-six-inch mail receptacle.

Creating the appearance that you are bigger than you really are has been the quest of the self-employed for decades. Computers and the Internet have made the task easier, but my recollection of how impressed I was with EWN's address reminds me of the power of perception.

While I've wanted to appear as a player among players, there is a fine line I have not been willing to cross. It's the deliberately false perceptions that some businesses project that offend me and other people as well. At the 1999 National Speakers Association convention, Morley Safer and a crew from *60 Minutes* spent a week following Zig Ziglar, a member of the organization. They were getting footage for an upcoming segment on motivational speakers. All week, we saw Safer interviewing luminaries in the organization, the TV camera capturing every detail of the convention. When the show aired several months later, every member was notified and encouraged to tune in. That Sunday night, my husband, and I sat down to watch the program. In a slow pan of the crowd, I saw myself for a full second and a half attentively watching the speaker. I was tickled, and Buddy started punching my arm in excitement. I got a few phone calls from friends who had spotted me, too. But the best response came in an e-mail from my colleague Susan Keane Baker. She laughingly suggested that I rewrite my promotional materials to include the phrase "as seen on *60 Minutes*." Companies have done much more than that to publicize themselves.

※   ※   ※

LESSON 44
Until they say, "Never call us again!", don't give up. Keep calling.

Paper House Productions has been my favorite greeting card company for many years. It sells die-cut photographic images of American icons such as the Chrysler Building, Harley-Davidson motorcycles, and Elvis, as well as cats, babies, flowers, and fruit. From the first time I saw Paper House's iconic cards in a museum shop, I visualized having images of my eggs as part of the line. In 1988 I sent a mock-up of an enlarged photograph of one of my eggs, die-cut and fashioned into a greeting card. A production assistant showed polite interest. I sent her a collection of slides for future consideration. A year passed.

We missed the Easter season, but I persevered. I went to the National Stationery Show at the Javits Convention Center in New York City to meet the owner of Paper House and introduce myself. He, too, showed interest and asked me to send three of my decorated eggs for him to photograph. We were getting closer. Six more months passed before he processed the images, but they didn't quite satisfy him. Disheartened, I waited another year before pursuing him again.

After completing some new designs I was excited about, I sent off another set of slides. We got further this time. We got into a licensing negotiation over the telephone. I mentioned the percentage I wanted, and the owner retorted, "Who do you think you are—the Wizard of Oz?" I was so dumbfounded by this comment that I remained silent for a long time. Then I hung up the phone.

A few months later, I was shopping at a local stationery store and passed the Paper House display. I noticed its *Wizard of Oz* collection— die-cut images of Dorothy, the ruby slippers, and the Tin Man, Scarecrow, and Lion—and realized the owner was being more literal than figurative. I renewed my campaign. More images sent. More trips to the Javits Center that yielded nothing.

In 1996 my book *Decorating Eggs* was published. I was so proud of it that I thought, "Now I'm going to be really famous. Paper House will regret that they didn't team up with me." So I sent the company a copy of my book, earmarked several pages featuring my favorite egg designs, and enclosed a note that read, "Last chance!" I refer to that as my what-the-hell marketing strategy.

Three days later, the firm called and ordered two of my designs. In 1997, nine years after my first letter to Paper House, my eggs were featured in its catalog in a row of notecards right next to Fabergé's.

※　※　※

LESSON 45
What you call "it" matters.

While I was in Charleston, South Carolina, one weekend, I wandered into an inviting shop called Worthwhile. There was a beautifully detailed white cotton shirtwaist in the window that caught my eye and drew me in. I suspected the price tag would be pretty detailed, too. I was right. It was $429.

I told the salesgirl how charmed I was by the dress. "Oh, that *piece* is designed by Gary Graham. We have several more *pieces* by him in the back."

Piece. As opposed to dress. Somehow it elevated it. I was no longer looking at clothing. I was viewing art. It altered the experience. I was drawn in, as to a museum show. I couldn't get it out of my head, although the pricing and small-size-only availability cured that urge.

The takeaway from this incident was the brilliance and simplicity of a trained sales staff and quality copywriting. A writer had developed the formidable skill of turning something that goes on your back into an experience for the shopper. Part of the overhead of a designer like Graham is paying for that service. No wonder the "piece" was so expensive.

Not long after the Charleston lesson it was driven home again that customers will niche our business in their minds with a single word or phrase. We business owners can help control what that word is. Witness the magnificent catalog I received from Mitchells, a high-end store near my town that was celebrating fifty years in business. Mitchells carries Armani, Ralph Lauren, Jimmy Choo, and many other elite designers. The store is elegant, the prices high. The sales staff is abundant and ever-present. Shopping there is up-close and personal. You know you're in good hands.

The Mitchell family is respected and loved in the community. What one word did they choose to represent themselves? Hugs! Hugs? Yes. Their catalog cover said in the boldest type: 50 Years of Hugs.

Jack Mitchell wrote the book *Hug Your Customers* a few years ago to rave reviews and sold-out editions. He now lectures worldwide on the subject of customer care. The family's stories of personal service are legendary.

If you'd asked me what word I would use to describe Mitchells, I'm sure I would have come up with something different. But I so admire how the family positioned themselves that I have continued to spread their word. That's the best marketing there is—getting others to tell your story for you.

※　※　※

CHAPTER 5

Control Systems, Gadgets, and Gizmos

(Before They Control You)

While I'd prefer that we compute time in dog years, the twenty-first century is relentlessly moving the hands of our clocks at warp speed. A Web usability strategist—those didn't exist when I started my business in the '70s—told me that my 2010 site looked "tired." Although it still felt brand new, the design created four years earlier was a lifetime ago by today's digital standards.

I remember when people in the business community would gently inquire if you had a fax machine so they might transmit a document that way. Those days of polite inquiry are gone. Now it is assumed that if you are in business, you are connected in every available mode of communication possible.

There is no predicting where our technology revolution will take us. But the willingness and enthusiasm to go for the ride are essentials for success.

LESSON 46

Getting advice from an expert is critical. You'll save time and money.

Even back in the early '70s, when everything seemed so much simpler, purchasing machinery was a major event. My husband and I took some of our wedding money to Bloomingdale's to invest in a hand-held calculator, an innovative piece of equipment that had recently come on the market. You have to put this in perspective. Pocket calculators costing $3.99 were not yet hanging off the racks at Staples. Staples didn't exist. Only department stores sold such equipment. We invested $80 in a Texas Instruments model—a significant amount of money in 1972. Similarly, in the 1980s, when fax machines became popular, we went again as a couple—this time to Staples—to decide what size, design, and function we needed, and which model we wanted to buy.

Before making a major tech purchase, I consult somebody for information, confirmation, or expertise. Ads and literature confuse me. I need to hear from a specialist exactly what I'm buying and how it will serve me. Then I make my decision. All my choices have made my business more efficient and competitive.

My friend Rick Wetzel is one such authority. As a developer for Apple Computer, he walked me through the purchase of my first Macintosh computer. We talked about the size of the monitor, the design of the keyboard, plus the printer and cables. Two weeks later, when it all got delivered, assembled, and plugged in, I called Rick in a panic. "Nothing's happening," I wailed. Calmly Rick looked at the invoice to see if everything we had ordered was on there. It turned out that a teensy-weensy detail had been overlooked. We had forgotten to order the hard drive. Who knew?

Seven computer purchases later—I'm now on my fourth laptop—I still seek consultation on the latest and greatest machinery. There is too much information for one entrepreneur to comprehend. I prefer using experts to help me weed through gigabytes, analog versus digital, and roaming versus long distance. I want to spend my precious time doing what I do best—coaching, writing, and talking about entrepreneurship.

I have found these experts through networking and meeting a variety of people in my associations. Most of the time these acquaintances and friends will provide the advice I need at no cost. It's one of the perks of being in a network—sharing expertise. My colleagues' generous spirits and wealth of information are the most reliable sources I have found.

※　※　※

LESSON 47
You don't hurt anyone's feelings when you toss bulk mail.

My friend Carol was desperate and sent out an SOS. She was suffering from an inability to throw things out. When I arrived on the scene, her dining room table was covered from end to end (and about three inches deep) with mail, mostly unopened. I announced that our goal was to process everything that day. I chose the "rapid gross sort" method for Carol, placing each item in one of four categories: toss, act, read, or file. As we approached each piece with these intentions, identifying items that had to be tossed was easy. She didn't have to do anything after she tossed them in the wastebasket. The "act" decision was harder. We made a tickler file, arranged by the date she had to pay bills or answer correspondence. Items to be read were divided into catalogs, magazines, and brochures. Each had a different folder. The "file" pile became the basis of her to-do list and remained manageable because the pile was not that big.

My friend did not become as ruthless as I am. I'm at the point where I barely look at anything without a first-class stamp. If it's bulk mail, I don't want to spend my time looking at it. Carol had too much compassion for direct marketers. For instance, she had received a sample America Online disk and wanted to keep it. I asked her if she was unhappy with her current Internet provider. She confessed she wasn't actually online yet. In fact, she was still deciding what kind of computer to buy. I assured her that she would be receiving demo disks or CDs weekly and that she could let go of this particular one.

She was still in a place I had once occupied—the "maybe someday" place that is nonproductive and keeps us stuck, overwhelmed with stacks of paper. No one enjoys sitting at a cluttered desk. When space is cleared, creative juices have room to flow. Carol's energy and enthusiasm mounted as her dining room table became increasingly more visible. Like me, she felt the psychological weight of all that unopened mail lifting off her shoulders.

Dealing promptly and efficiently with incoming mail each day is a challenge for every entrepreneur. Sometimes calling a friend in to help tame the paper tiger is the best way to get out from under.

※　※　※

LESSON 48
Organizing yourself helps you get to the questions that need answers.

You know the women (I'm convinced that men don't do this) who clean their houses before the cleaning lady comes? I took a page out of their book when I made an appointment to work with a professional organizer. We can take the people we mentor only as far as we have gone ourselves. The afternoon I spent at Carol's, helping her clear her cluttered table, motivated me to do my own office cleaning. I already knew how to sort my mail and files. I needed to create new systems and called on a pro so that I could get to the next level.

I had several logjams I couldn't figure out. How do I keep all those wires on my desk—from my phone, computer cables, printer, and head-set—under control? Where do I put my business card contacts that are multiplying daily? How do I organize the various components of my promotional kits—publicity, testimonial letters, and marketing pieces—so they remain within arm's reach without overwhelming me?

I began the job a week before the professional organizer was to show up. I wanted to make the best use of her time, so I plowed through my entire office, drawer by drawer, cabinet by cabinet, so that I could produce a detailed list we would study together. The initial job worked wonders. It helped me formulate the questions I needed to ask. In addition, by going through all of my files, I got rid of years' worth of unnecessary paper. I discarded software and accompanying literature for a computer we had given to charity three years and one platform ago. I noticed multiple spiral-bound notebooks cluttering my desk. They contained computer questions and answers, daily records of my income and expenses, a gratitude list I'd been keeping for months. Could I eliminate or combine any of these?

My professional organizer streamlined all of my operations in a few well-spent hours. She suggested a five-section notebook for the contents of the several smaller ones. I purchased a stand that raised my phone to a new height and gave me a place below to store its accessories. A literature bin with twelve slots could hold my promotional materials and my data entry additions within easy reach. Best of all, I now have a clear head. I no longer have the physical clutter that used to cloud my thinking and hamper my activity. Not having those little scraps, wires, and distractions allowed me to focus more clearly.

After she had completed her magic, I realized what really inspires me. It's not a trip to the museum, although that often works. It's not hearing a motivational speech, even though those help me reframe old thoughts and ideas. What really, really gets me inspired is a clean desk.

All the time, effort, and expense required to build systems for creating and maintaining a clean desk are worth it. Bringing in a professional has become an annual ritual for me, and I still organize as best I can before she comes.

※　※　※

LESSON 49
Break down the items on your to-do list into manageable pieces.

I've applied the principle "chunking it down" to my business on a regular basis. As soon as I write down a goal, such as "Create a short-term coaching group for women in transition," I can feel my heart start to race in fear and anticipation. My gremlins start saying things like "Yeah, but how are you going to get people to come?" and "Not in this economy!"

My first therapist introduced me to the phrase "chunking it down" many years ago. She said that although she thoroughly enjoyed entertaining friends, she would feel overwhelmed at the prospect of making a meal for fifteen people. So she learned how to chunk it down. She would break up the work of a dinner party into its multiple tasks (chunks) and then begin one of the chunks. The party became manageable when all she had to do at any given point in time was chop carrots for a salad.

The first thing I do when I'm thinking of taking on something difficult is to jot down all the tasks on a road map that will take me there. Then I can convert this map into a list of things to do that gets plugged into my daily schedule.

When Linda Koe and I worked together to create an independent exhibit of our work, we mind-mapped together, creating categories such as locating a venue, getting PR, designing an invitation, finding a mailing house, and hiring workers to assist at the event. Each of these categories had subcategories, such as finding a graphic artist to design the invitation and researching where to send our press releases.

One category, producing the work we would sell (inventory), required different activities for each of us. Linda needed to search for vintage quilts to resell. I had to make hundreds of pieces of art to sell. First I made a list of everything I wanted to produce for the show—decorated eggs, holiday ornaments, pins, earrings, and cuff links made from eggshells. Then I took a calendar and looked at how many days I had to prepare. I blocked out any day when I had commitments that would rule out studio time. Then I began plugging my production list into the available days. I blocked out time on the calendar to craft each piece. I assigned the creation of a log cabin-patterned egg to Tuesday morning. I would also have time that day to outline four egg ornaments. On Wednesday I planned to make four Ukrainian deer pins and two pairs of matching earrings. And so I went, chunking down my list into manageable daily activities. Once I had relegated the entire list to specific days, I took a look at my filled calendar and felt a sense of relief. It was doable. And there was plenty of time to spare.

A frequently asked question at many of my exhibits was "How do you find the time?" We all have the same twenty-four hours per day. The most important aspect of chunking it down is that when the task shows up on your calendar, you do it then without procrastination. It's the cumulative effect of putting off tasks that makes them seem insurmountable. Chunking them down is a success formula not only for socializing but also for business events and lifelong achievement.

※　※　※

LESSON 50
Choose when and where to conduct business.

While I'm not an advocate of doing business 24/7 or bringing your BlackBerry to the lunch table, I do believe that you can operate from anywhere these days. Good friends had been planning a weeklong vacation to Florida. One of them had recently lost his job and thought he might need to stay back in Connecticut to make phone calls, follow up on leads, and suffer.

A wise colleague of mine has a penchant for saying, "I carry my office in my pocket," meaning that wherever he is, he's open for business. It could be the car, an evening at home, or actually at his desk with file folders in hand. He is 100 percent reachable, if he wants to be.

Another associate suggested that it would be a great opportunity for our mutual friend to learn how to do business on the beach, as she has done in the past. I say, "Ditto!" A well-planned and prepaid (!) vacation is essential to our well-being. It would be deprivation to deny yourself this opportunity.

I do want to advocate for the flip side of the availability issue, too. And that is to choose occasions when you are consciously unavailable, like dinnertime. During a weekend Relationships Coaching program, I intentionally turned off my phone throughout the day. I've taken weeklong vacations when my outgoing messages—both e-mail and phone—said I would respond when I got back. And, on a rare occasion, I have been at a meal with a friend and announced before we sat down that I needed to have my phone on should that newspaper editor call about the press release I just sent.

The important piece here is that you get to decide. Choose your priorities. Take a stand for what's most important. There is room for both. You run the office. Don't let the office run you.

※　※　※

LESSON 51

Shutting out the business world is essential for your personal well-being.

My father didn't curse often, but he inevitably would when the phone rang during supper. This was the '50s and '60s—before answering machines, voice mail, or even off buttons for the ringers. He hated that anyone from the outside world could disturb our family's peace, and we had no control. Today we do have control, but oh so many more invasions into our domestic lives. My friend Linda is new to computers (I know, I know), having resisted allowing them into her life until a few months ago. She confessed to me that she finds e-mail invading her life. "*You* have to choose when to respond or it can consume you," she said.

The rest of us are like those frogs in a pot of water where the heat is being gradually turned up. They don't notice they're getting killed. Linda, who jumped into the boiling caldron, immediately "got" that it's too hot to survive. Smart lady!

I allow myself a few limited time periods to deal with e-mail— twenty-minute blocks of time using a timer. Without that limitation, I'm too easily drawn into the vortex that is cyberspace and can't get out. Anything that doesn't get dealt with during those prescribed times gets saved until the next allotted slot.

After seven days of being entirely unplugged while on a spa vacation one year, I appreciated how sacred time is and how vital it is to set our own limits and respect them. I emerged from that trip more renewed and invigorated than from any other vacation ever.

※　※　※

LESSON 52
Enter the technology waters at your own pace, but do enter.

My kids are tweeting their hearts out. They were born to this techno-logical age. In nursery school, Laura was in the dress-up corner playing grocery store and scanning bananas over the toy cash register. I didn't understand why she was waving the fruit over the keys in that particular way rather than just punching in the dollars and cents. Our next trip to Stew Leonard's, the world's largest dairy store, revealed the answer as the checkout clerk there used the same motion. "Smart kid, my daugh-ter," I thought. She observed a behavior I had been oblivious to.

I'm on the learning curve. We baby boomers have adapted to answer-ing machines, computers, cellphones, and the like, each time protesting "Who needs that?" before adopting and proclaiming their benefits.

I know I will continue to master new technology and apps, now that I know what an app is. I know that it's important. I know I will make great connections and learn lots. But in the moment of introduction, I don't get it and I am whiny and annoyed. However, I recognize that that's my style and move forward anyway. I take Twitter lessons via tele-classes and watch YouTube videos to learn more and keep up.

In my morning meditation book *Courage to Change*, a daily passage ends with a quote by Confucius: It does not matter how slowly you go so long as you do not stop.

Unstoppable is my middle name.

※　※　※

LESSON 53
A guiding hand eases the transition from fear to action.

When chatting with a friend about our hectic schedules, she characterized her current to-do list like this:

- Easy
- Easy
- Hard
- Scary

We both laughed, but my thoughts immediately turned to the most frightening thing on my own to-do list. For some time, starting a blog had number one status in the "scary" category. Oh sure, I knew it was a good idea, that creating an online community was important. I was aware that my business would benefit from regular exchanges with clients and colleagues. But because starting a blog was new for me and scary, not to mention how exposed I would feel, it remained on my "still not done" list. For a year.

Then, after all that procrastination, I found help. That's the key ingredient for me when I'm afraid and don't know how to take the next step. My ears were open to hear the name of a techno whiz who spoke at an Entrepreneurial Woman's Network event. A mastermind group colleague heard Lena West and, knowing how long I'd wanted to get started and hadn't, recommended her to me. After excellent instruction, handholding, and patience from Lena, I squeezed my eyes shut, pinched my nose tight, and leapt into the blogosphere.

It was exciting. My first post went up in May 2008. I saw via my dashboard stats that more than a hundred people read that first entry. Many commented. The second post flowed easily from there. There's so much to talk about in my business. I began to kick myself that I should have done it sooner.

Actually, the timing was perfect. It always is.

※　※　※

CHAPTER 6
Relationship Building – One Relationship at a Time

There's a lesson learned in every relationship I encounter. My periodontist promptly responded to a written complaint I had made, letting him know that his Novocain shot was more painful than any I had previously experienced. He personally phoned me to apologize. I've been his patient for more than twenty-five years as a result.

A new acquaintance repeatedly ignored my voice mail and e-mail messages after her suggestion that we get together. I see her events publicized regularly and am curious how she manages her affiliations.

A workshop co-leader knows when my spirit is flagging and patiently allows me to find my way back to the joy of our work. The safety in that bond will keep me partnering with him for years to come.

What I know is that each relationship is forged independently, regardless of reputation or status. My formula for success is bringing my heart to each encounter and finding the connection between us.

LESSON 54

Whenever you receive a compliment, simply say, "Thank you."

Gracious acknowledgment of a compliment, in business or in your personal life, shows that you respect the giver and that you realize you're worthy of such praise. When my youngest child was in third grade, she agreed to go on her first overnight field trip. I envisioned a teary farewell the morning of the expedition. We got a call before we were about to leave, asking if we'd pick up a classmate of Laura's en route. I asked my daughter's permission, thinking that she might have wanted the emotional moment of departure to be more private, but she was OK with it.

On the way to Caitlin's, I said, "It was very sweet of you to include Caitlin this morning." Laura answered, "It fills me with joy to have her." I was so moved by her magnanimous spirit I practically shouted, "Laura, you are joy!" She recoiled in her seat and said, "Oooooohhh, Mom, please." I immediately went into a lecture mode. I wanted her to understand and value praise—a lesson I had learned the hard way. I told her that story. One day, when I was at a show exhibiting my work, a customer came to my booth and admired the sweater I was wearing. I looked down to see what top I had on, tugged at the garment with my thumbs and forefingers, and said, "Loehmann's," a premium designer discount chain. She was crestfallen. I had diminished her words by rejecting the compliment.

"So," I told Laura, "from that moment forward, I changed my behavior. Whenever I receive a compliment, I take a deep breath, sometimes I even put my hands over my heart—taking in the words—and say thank you. Do you want to try that again, honey?" She nodded. I repeated, "Laura, you are joy," and she nodded as a way of thanking me. She looked down at her jacket, fingered the lapel, coyly looked up at me with a twinkle in her eye, and said, "Loehmann's."

※　※　※

LESSON 55

Be open to new encounters. Be careful not to prejudge people.

I believe in serendipity. My preferred hotel had been fully booked so I ended up at another hotel. The next morning, I found a table in the dining area where I could quietly read my book and relax over coffee before the day's event. The breakfast crowd that morning was large, so I wasn't surprised when a woman asked if she could sit at my table. I made a conscious decision to set aside my book and find out why the universe had placed this particular individual in my space. She was older than I, exotically coiffed, and bedecked with strands of beads.

"What brings you to Massachusetts?" I asked.

"I'm here for my granddaughter's middle school graduation," she replied. I was hoping for something more interesting.

"And what brings you here?" she graciously added. Aah. At least it wouldn't be all about her. It's important to note two things here. Only two sentences into the conversation and already the judgments were flooding my brain. I'd invalidated this woman's role on earth after one sentence and then readmitted her because she'd shown interest in me.

"I'm here for a meeting of the National Speakers Association. I'm a professional speaker," I replied.

"Oh, what do you speak about?" She was becoming more interesting by the minute.

"I'm an artist. I talk about turning your passion into a business."

"I'm an artist, too," she said. Hat of judgment back on my head.

"Really?" Many people think they're artists. I decided to start with the all-important question that divides the amateurs from the pros. "Do you sell your work?"

"Yes, I do."

"Oh, really. Where?" Still trying to find out if she was for real or a wannabe.

"New York," she said. Buffalo, I thought. Anyone can sell art in Buffalo.

"Manhattan," she clarified. "Fifty-seventh Street." I reframed the situation. While my first instinct was to help a naïve aspirant to the arts, the tables were now turned and I was in a position to benefit from a New York artist's experience.

"What kind of work do you do?" I am not very current on the New York art scene, but I hoped to show a modicum of intelligence about her field.

"I paint very large canvases with autobiographical materials, then add stitches to the canvases."

Even though my knowledge of contemporary artists is slim, the minute she said "stitches," a bell went off in my head. "May I ask your name?"

"Faith Ringgold."

OMIGOD! The one contemporary artist whom I really admire and whose work I had seen dozens of times in *The Crafts Report* and *Fiberarts*—two trade magazines for people in the arts—was Faith Ringgold.

"Would you mind waiting here for a minute? I would love to show you what I do." I ran to the car, where I had packed my first book and my decorated eggs. I brought them in and placed them before her like an offering at the altar. Faith proceeded to leaf through my book page by page, commenting, smiling, and appreciating my work.

Then I opened the box of eggs so that she could see the real things. I carry them in a cardboard egg carton, just the way you would pick them up in a supermarket. I always enjoy watching people's reactions when they see these miniature works.

Although her eyes and her smile delighted me, it was the question that followed that would remain with me: "How much are they a dozen?" No one had ever asked me that question. When I began the craft more than twenty-five years ago, my eggs sold for $8 apiece. With experience, great press, and increased self-esteem, the price had escalated to $250 per egg. The calculator in my head rapidly multiplied that amount times twelve. "Three thousand dollars," I replied. She said, "If I were you, I would only offer them by the dozen, and I would sell them in a glass egg carton." Brilliant! A million-dollar idea.

Had I stayed at the first hotel, and had I chosen to read my book and not deigned to go outside my comfort zone to initiate a conversation with a stranger, I would have missed what turned out to be one of the most exciting and profitable encounters in my career. The more open I stay to what the universe plants in my path, the more spectacular the journey.

※   ※   ※

LESSON 56
Go! You might meet somebody!

Typically at a craft show, customers entered my booth, got a feel for my work, and often took out their eyeglasses from a pocket or purse to examine my work more closely. At a festival in a nearby town, I observed one customer's less typical behavior. After glancing at the designs on the front of my brooches, she flipped them over and peered at the reverse side. After spending several minutes doing this, she asked me what material I was using to fill the concave areas of the eggshell.

I went into a detailed explanation of epoxy—a resin that is complicated to use, requiring precise measurement and application. She nodded. She owned a company that packaged epoxy in pre-measured units. They would be much easier to use and would improve production of my eggs.

Because she enjoyed my work, she offered to swap her epoxy for my jewelry. I accepted her offer and for years exchanged my products for hers. It was a mutually satisfying and financially rewarding relationship.

I know when I show up—participate in a craft show, attend a networking event, or simply follow through on a commitment to have lunch with a friend—something always happens, and the universe will meet me.

※   ※   ※

LESSON 57
Build your reputation one customer at a time.

Once I ordered a richly patterned wool challis scarf from a catalog company. When my shipment arrived, I was disappointed to find the scarf was made of rayon. The colors were not as vivid, and the fabric lacked the texture I had anticipated. I thought I was going to have an unpleasant time over the phone with the customer service department, but I left the conversation not only satisfied but also astonished by the representative's attitude.

She asked me, "How can we make you happy?" What a concept—to ask the customer what she wanted. I told the representative I was disappointed because I had ordered the scarf to wear as an accessory while exhibiting my work that weekend. "Why don't you wear the one we sent you and then return it to us after the show?" the representative suggested.

I felt the company was really taking care of me.

I want my customers to feel the same way. So many businesses act defensively when a customer complains. I had been guilty of that myself. Although I've mentally blocked out the specifics of past experiences, I still remember giving the evil eye to one customer who was browsing in my booth. She held up a blackened finger to show me that the epoxy I had used on the back of a brooch hadn't dried sufficiently. I wanted to blame her. Call it immaturity, human instinct, or self-defense, anything but customer service. I resented her calling attention to my inadequacy so much I didn't even offer her a tissue to clean her finger.

Another example of a company that knows how to provide customer service is Stew Leonard's, the world's largest dairy store. It is just two miles from my home, so I get to witness its operations on a frequent basis. At the store's entrance is an enormous rock into which is chiseled the company's two-rule philosophy: The customer is always right. If the customer is wrong, go back to rule number 1.

I remember the first time I consciously tried this approach. A woman who had bought one of my pins called me a week or two after its purchase. "Some of the shiny coating on my pin has chipped off," she said. "No problem," I replied. "I'll send you another one and enclose a return mailer for yours." That didn't hurt too much. It so happened I had a duplicate piece in my inventory and could easily replace the damaged pin. I felt that I had handled a customer complaint gracefully.

One month later, the same customer phoned again. "Jane, I'm very upset to tell you this, but I'm noticing a similar occurrence on the replacement pin. The shiny coating is peeling off." My instinct was to bark, "What are you doing to my pins?" But, because I had played the role of frustrated consumer many times myself, I wanted to handle her complaint with grace and ease. I explained that I had no more of that design in stock but I would be happy to make a new one and send it to her. The epoxy fillings and coatings each take twenty-four hours to set, so the process is labor-intensive and time-consuming. But I had vowed to make my customers happy. Within a week, I had completed the new version of her order and shipped it off. She called me as soon as she received it. "You have the best customer service I've ever experienced," she said.

I had no idea what to expect when I followed through on my commitment to take care of my customers. She helped me learn a valuable lesson. I create my reputation as a business owner one customer at a time, the same way that Stew Leonard and the catalog company create theirs. Caring for each and every customer is an indispensable duty.

Good customer service benefited me in another way as well. As a result of that experience, I called the epoxy manufacturer to find out how to get better adhesion in the future. With the information I got, I became a better, more informed artisan.

※　※　※

LESSON 58
Listen to customers' complaints. It will pay off.

"You want to write off your trip to Universal Studios?" my accountant asked incredulously. "Yes," I replied. "While our intention was to have fun there, it turned into an opportunity to do some research."

My husband and I went there on a hot, dry summer day—at least ninety degrees in the shade. Lines at the park snaked around the maze of holding pens. Every ride we passed was equally mobbed, so we chose the "E.T." line. Most of the great theme parks have figured out how to keep folks happy during the long waits. Discreetly installed sprinklers sprayed us with water, not heavy enough to drench us and our clothes, just a delicate spray.

"Can you imagine the courageous employee who made that suggestion?" I asked. I pictured the company meeting where one disgruntled employee after another complained about how poorly treated they were by customers who had grown hostile in the long, sweltering lines. "Why don't we just pour water on 'em and cool 'em down?" I also knew that it must have taken months of analysis, planning, and implementation.

The ride was fun, but it was the fabulous customer service that stayed with me. What lengths do I go to for my customers? What are their concerns? What didn't they like? I think about details like this in my work all the time. When I started making pins out of eggshells, I attached the pin backs and earring posts with sticky pads. Too many were returned with that piece missing. My customers were gracious because they loved the jewelry, but I knew I needed to improve the pins. I began embedding the pin backs and posts in a second layer of epoxy, increasing the production time by twenty-four hours but creating a permanent solution. Of course, new buyers don't even notice the improvement. That's good customer service.

Much as I dislike hearing criticism, no matter how warmly expressed, I now regard it as an opportunity to keep my customers cool.

※ ※ ※

LESSON 59

It is important to thank everyone who has helped you in significant ways.

When we were growing up, my brother teasingly referred to the family's Dow Joy Averages—the measuring device for how much credit we brought to our parents on a given day. It made me hyper-aware of who owed me what and whom I owed what. When I teach strategies for growing your business, I always include thanking people who have helped you in significant ways. I don't mean thanking people who hold a door open for you. I do mean showing your gratitude when someone gives you a great lead, referral, or piece of advice, or has contributed something that has helped you grow your business.

Although most people don't keep score, they do have an unconscious accounting system that registers if there are still "open emotional accounts receivable." You can withdraw only as much as you have put in.

Once I was telling a class in a college about the evolution of my business. One of the students was interested in the construction business. As I had a friend in the construction business, I suggested that the student call him. About six weeks later, I phoned my friend to check out an upcoming conference. When that student answered the phone, I was very surprised and asked what he was doing there. He replied, "Oh, I'm working for Mark now." Neither one had acknowledged that I had put together their relationship. All that was required was the simplest acknowledgment via e-mail—"thanks so much for the referral"—or a quick phone call. That little touch can work wonders and removes the burden of an open account.

※ ※ ※

LESSON 60
Stay focused on the people who are buying your products.

I often go to a nearby day spa and have learned a great deal from the owner, Noel. She nurtured her customers, and they responded by caring about her and her spa. I asked how she started her business. She answered simply, "The owner of a beauty parlor handed me a broom and said, 'First you will sweep hair. Then you cut hair.' "

Noel is one of several successful women who have inspired me. Her humble beginnings, her spiritual approach, and her spa's implementation of feng shui principles—everything she said interested me. As a marketing strategy, she gave a $5 gift certificate to each customer and offered a reduced price on haircuts for customers who made appointments at hours when the spa is quieter. I took her up on both offers. I used the $5 for my first haircut, and since I don't work a 9-to-5 job, I got my hair cut on Tuesday mornings to save even more money.

The spa is also very efficient. You can tell from the moment you walk in. The first time I went to the spa, the receptionist consulted the computer. "I see you're here for the first time. Let me show you where we keep our smocks." And she escorted me to the dressing room. On the way, she asked, "While you're waiting for your shampoo, can I bring you a cup of coffee, tea, herbal tea, or hot water with lemon?" She made me feel pampered, treasured, wonderful.

A bit later when I emerged with my smock on, a young man dressed in black approached. "I'll be giving you your shampoo." He, too, escorted me to my chair. Once there, he asked, "May I massage your neck and shoulders while we wait for the water to warm up?" I felt like a goddess.

I haven't even mentioned the interior design of the salon. The layout is absolutely functional. At the same time, it is breathtakingly beautiful with a unique array of building materials, textures, and fabrics. It makes you feel good to be there.

The haircut was equal to every other part of the experience. For Noel's $5 investment, I became a regular customer. She further endeared herself to me when I had a problem. After two of my appointments had been canceled because my haircutter was ill, I asked for a substitute. I was offered a handsome young man.

I arrived early so that I could check him out before he cut my hair. He had a very attractive blond woman in his chair and was fussing over every strand on her head, smiling and laughing. I couldn't wait to sit in his chair. When it was my turn, I offered him a photograph of myself showing the cut I wanted. He acknowledged it with a nod and proceeded to work. Throughout the thirty minutes I was in his chair, he did not say one word to me. I felt invisible, unimportant, and embarrassed.

When I paid the receptionist, she asked me how everything was. "Not as good as usual," I muttered almost inaudibly.

"Someone will call you," she responded immediately. (Noel's staff is very sensitive to customer complaints.) The next day I received a call from a person on the staff. She listened to me vent. The haircut the stylist had given me was fine. It's just that it wasn't how I like to be treated.

"We would like to make it up to you," she said. "Can we give you a complimentary visit?"

"No," I protested. "You've already exceeded my expectations by hearing me vent. I'm OK now. Thank you." I felt important and valued as a customer. What impressed me even more was that within a week of that follow-up call I received a handwritten letter from Noel promising to make my next appointment "nothing short of perfect." Every detail of Noel's business, from the towel rack in the ladies' room to the talent of her practitioners, has her personal stamp.

※　※　※

LESSON 61

Whether your audience is one person or a thousand, speak as though they are your most important clients.

When I considered attending a seminar on business law, it looked about as exciting as reading the encyclopedia. I knew I could get some interesting information out of it if I delved, but who wanted to make the effort? However, it was a requirement for the business owner's course I was taking with the American Woman's Economic Development Corporation. So I dragged myself into New York City to attend the first session.

Even though it was required, I was the only member of my class to show up. Still, instructor Jill Botway spoke as if I were the most important client or audience she had ever addressed. Her session was riveting. Jill was a brilliant, successful attorney whose legal team had never lost a case. What I remember most about her session, now decades later, was the story she told me about the Mianus River bridge, which had collapsed near my home. The bridge is on a span of Interstate 95, a highly trafficked artery in the Northeast. It was unthinkable that a piece of a major highway could simply cave in. It caused hideous traffic congestion until repairs were finished a year later.

Jill was the lawyer for a woman whose car had plunged into the Mianus River when the road fell away. As Jill capsulized the issue, "When you're pushing a wheelchair holding your twenty-three-year-old client into the courtroom and it's her against the big-business contractors who built the bridge, she's going to win the sympathy of the court." The case, which ended with a settlement, produced the largest award in Connecticut's history at that time.

Later, when not one soul showed up for a class I was scheduled to conduct in a store, it was Jill's professionalism at the seminar that I remembered. I did the right thing. I invited the manager to round up any employees who might be interested in the material and presented my talk to them. Without Jill's model, I might have behaved in a different way—I might have complained to the owner of the store about her store's advertising campaign or let my disappointment show to my new audience, the employees who decided to attend.

※　※　※

CHAPTER 7

Real Pros Don't Go It Alone – Find Support and Accountability

Imitation may be the sincerest form of flattery, but it's also a plan of action for becoming the success you want to be. I don't mean copying anyone else's style or tagline. I do mean following in the footsteps of a mentor or role model who will lead you through the paces of your specific industry.

First I observed the behaviors and disciplines of craftspeople I admired, took the courses they took, and noticed where they exhibited and advertised. Later I joined the National Speakers Association and the International Coach Federation to learn from those peers.

Only in my first year or two as an egg decorator did I mistakenly think I was supposed to know all the answers. It was lonely and unrewarding. Since those early days, I have sought help in every aspect of my business, from hiring an assistant to glue labels onto gift boxes to creating a business page on Facebook. If I had to master every facet of business on my own, I would never have time to profit from my unique talent.

LESSON 62

It's your business, and you are in charge of every aspect of it, even the jobs you delegate.

Brian Tracy, creator of *The Psychology of Achievement*, has a mantra: "I am responsible." It was one of my least favorite things to hear on his tapes. In fact, I hated the sound of those words. They took away all my excuses, self-pity, self-righteousness, and my favorite face-saving device, blaming others. Of course, I also knew that he was dead right, which is why I particularly resented those words. For example, following a wildly successful craft show, I was calculating all my sales, including the charge receipts, when I noticed that several charges had not been through the credit card swipe machine. This meant that these sales would be invalid, because I didn't have a record of the customers' card numbers. I realized those receipts had been processed by the assistant I had hired to help me at the show and was furious because it represented hundreds of dollars in lost sales.

My first response normally would have been to call this woman and vent my anger and frustration. Then I began to consider Brian's mantra. How could I possibly be responsible for her obvious blunder? The answer dawned slowly. I knew where I had erred. I had not taken sufficient time to review the processing of credit cards with her. I had not walked her through the use of the swipe machine. I had not had the foresight to create a simple instruction sheet for her so that it would be a foolproof task. I was indeed responsible.

Jane Fonda's words "no pain, no gain" do work. But why is it that the only way I learn these lessons is when they cost me money?

*   *   *

LESSON 63

Before you hire people to provide special services, get a recommendation from a person who is familiar with their abilities.

When I needed a dentist, I asked my friend Betsy for the name of hers. I knew it was a safe bet because she was so thorough in whatever she tackled. I knew she would have done all the research. I was right. Her dentist became our family's painless and competent caregiver until he retired. I wish that there had been an egg-decorating Betsy in my business life—a vetted source I could go to for every referral I needed. Instead, I had to learn other methods for acquiring good help. I still haven't come up with a fail-safe solution.

A well-qualified, word-of-mouth referral is my preferred method for hiring any service provider. Seeking out sources used by successful friends and colleagues is the surest route to happy business relationships. Placing ads or getting secondhand referrals is a gamble.

When I wanted a new design for my booth at craft shows, I had two experiences that were costly and not satisfactory. I tried the referral method but didn't know the source well enough to trust his reliability. I asked a professor at a highly regarded professional school in New York City for the name of a student designer, and he told me about a woman— a student of his—who lived outside Manhattan.

She prepared a magnificent design that would use elegant yet inexpensive materials. Her design estimate was within my budget, and we made an agreement to work together. I was feeling proud of myself and cocky that this first attempt at hiring a designer was working so well. However, though this young woman was a creative genius, it turned out she was not all there mentally. After I had given her my deposit, her behavior verged on insanity. During the course of constructing the display, she became visibly pregnant and claimed virginal conception. Throughout our months working together, she continued to express bewilderment about her condition and how it came to be. My calls inquiring about her work on my design went unanswered. As my deadline approached, I began to panic. I had seen nothing yet. I ended up driving to her home, hours away, to monitor the progress. In the end, I used the display only one time because it was too bulky to transport and too difficult to erect by myself.

The next designer I hired came up with a more functional display, but his follow-through was sloppy and disappointing. I had to hold back some of his payment and confront him in order to get the display up to the quality we had agreed upon—it was a very unpleasant experience. That referral had been secondhand or thirdhand from someone who worked in the same building that housed his studio.

I prefer to talk about my successful hires because they are much less painful. For years, Mary Quinlan, the chair of the Norwalk High School art department, near my home in Norwalk, Connecticut, recommended one phenomenal art student after another. She understood the nature of the work I do and the delicate hands required to assist me. As her best students reached their senior year, she started looking over her juniors so she could keep me in production when my current worker graduated.

When Liz Wheeler, one of Mary's recommendations, was about to go off to college, I teased her by asking if she by any chance had a sister to take her place. She did. Rachel Wheeler was a sophomore at the time, and she worked in my studio for two years after Liz left. She was not only a terrific artist and helper, but also a brilliant English student who proofread my first book.

One of my best employees, Elizabeth Bullis-Wiese, recommended herself to me. A friend of mine had referred Elizabeth to do landscape work outside our house. While working in the yard, Elizabeth asked to peek in my studio to see what kind of work I did. As a part-time artist, she was intrigued and offered her services to me as an assistant. During her off-season, Elizabeth did production work for me for years.

Having an employee in my studio benefits me on many levels. First, my workload is less, and delegating tasks frees me to do what I do best.

Second, working at home alone can be extremely isolating. I lose my sense of reality and perspective. Having another person present with whom to discuss new ideas helps a lot. Getting a second opinion is invaluable, and having that capability at my disposal several hours a week is a necessary component of my success.

I've learned in my thirty-plus years in business that the best way to find help is through known connections—people in my classes or networks who understand the nature of my business. Second to a vetted referral is being excruciatingly careful in detailing the task at hand so that I and the person I am hiring are both clear on my expectations and how they will be carried out.

※　※　※

LESSON 64
Keep talking to various experts until you reach the perfect solution.

The life of every entrepreneur is filled with peaks and valleys that often occur on the same day, if not the same hour. It's the nature of owning your own business. The trick is to remember what the peaks looked like when you're in the valley. As I pursued Faith Ringgold's million-dollar idea for a "Dozen Eggs" in a glass carton, I peaked and dipped often. Initially I envisioned the eggs as similar to fine china. Those elegant designs on fine dinnerware that used to be painted by hand are now done almost exclusively with decals. Once I got over my prejudice about decals, I was able to accept the idea that they might prove useful in my work.

First, I tracked down a person who knew how to make decals. He was suggested by a friend. I drove to his shop in northern Connecticut and spoke to him at great length about producing decals and the transfer process. After I described the requirements, he referred me to an associate who worked closer to my home and had the sophisticated equipment I needed. I scheduled an appointment with his associate. He was intrigued by the idea of a collection of eggs and admired my designs. He took me on a tour of the premises and introduced me to the artisans he would involve in the project. I came home elated. I called in a progress report to my business coach, who was walking me through this undertaking. I had agreed to research three service providers but felt certain I'd already found the perfect person. She prodded me to check out at least one other vendor.

I dug into my Rolodex and called an art director who warned me to steer clear of the businessman I'd just met: "You've got to use our guy in New York. He's the best." So I scheduled an appointment to chat with her guy. He, too, liked the idea. Although he could also supply the decals, he thought it would be more viable to batik real chicken eggs using the traditional Ukrainian technique. He knew of a studio in the Far

East that could imitate my work so closely I wouldn't be able to tell the difference. I bought his idea along with his dismissal of his competitor in the decal business.

After anxiously waiting eight weeks to see the sample from overseas, I received a package with three beautiful Chinese boxes nestled in tissue paper. I eagerly lifted the lid off each box and recoiled in disappointment. The reproduction of my designs was grossly inaccurate, and the colors were not only mismatched—they were also hideous. I was sick to my stomach and called to tell him the deal was off.

Earlier in my career, I would have given up at this point, but I now have methods for dealing with these valleys. I used my coach, my mastermind group, and my friends to vent my frustrations to. And then I continued my quest. I believe that the reason the first two businesses didn't work was that a better option was waiting in the wings.

I called Artoria Limoges in New York City, the largest manufacturer of porcelain in the world. I knew and respected their artists' work, and originally had wanted them for the project but was too scared to approach them. Toughened by my previous attempts, I realized I had nothing to lose. Plus, I had gained a great deal of knowledge in those forays. Artoria loved the idea and helped me decide that painting my designs by hand on porcelain eggs that could be opened like boxes would be the method of choice. The Circle of Life Collection had its debut at the 2000 New York Gift Show, at the Javits Convention Center. It featured six of my quilt-patterned designs, hand-painted on egg-shaped porcelain boxes packaged and displayed in a clear carton.

※　※　※

LESSON 65
Choose the vendors who listen to you.

A salesman came to my home office one afternoon to pitch the benefits and features of his payroll service. I had called him because I was ready to delegate another time-consuming, yet essential, task of a business owner. He strode into my space, took a look around, and began to spout his company's services. "We work with a lot of small offices like yours; we have several one- and two-man operations."

"Actually," I corrected him, "this is a one-woman operation."

"Yeah, yeah, yeah," he agreed.

He continued to talk about the conveniences his company offered. I could make a toll-free call each week to report my payroll. I would speak to one of twelve employees or just leave my figures on a voice-mail recording. They would handle the rest.

"What if I always want to talk to the same person each time?"

"Oh, anyone at the company will be able to help you," he replied.

"Do you have some other business owners I might call for references, to see how it's working for them?"

"Sure, let me give you the names of some of the ten-man-or-fewer businesses I deal with." Somehow I had the feeling that he was not listening to my needs and was not even noticing what kind of company I was operating.

Fortunately, I had called two other payroll services that also sent out salesmen. I chose to work with the company whose owner came to see me. He asked me a lot of questions about my business and then addressed each of my concerns. I worked with him for many years and highly recommended his service to other entrepreneurs whether they were one-woman, one-man, or a slightly larger operation.

※ ※ ※

LESSON 66
Find people who can guide you toward your destiny.

I'm sure that some lucky folks out there knew from day one that they were going to be doctors, poets, or presidents. But for the rest of us, it helps to have friends who can guide us. I bumped into two mentors at my alma mater, Mount Holyoke College. We were required to take a variety of general education courses for a well-rounded liberal arts education. Among these general education requirements were eight credits in the arts. I selected classes in studio art and theater.

In an introductory theater course, I met Oliver Allyn, the department chair and stage design professor. After I'd been working backstage painting scenery for several weeks, the professor took me aside, placed his hand on my shoulder, and said, "I'd like to proselytize you. I want you to become a theater arts major." I didn't know how to react. Should I be insulted or pleased? Once he explained his intentions, I went back to my dorm to ponder the invitation. Looking back on that experience, it was the first time I remember any adult, other than my parents and my second-grade art teacher (who used to take me out of class to paint murals), taking an interest in my talents and me. I declared a double major of studio art and theater.

Jim Cavanaugh arrived in the theater department my senior year. He was well-known as a director. He made me property mistress for his first production on campus, *The Caucasian Chalk Circle*. As an upperclassman, I thought the job was beneath me—until I read the script and discovered that there were well over 100 props to collect and create, including bunraku (Japanese-style) puppets and an imaginary river.

He also invited me to design the logo for the production. He scheduled a trip to the printer and accompanied me there. The printer handed me a sheet of typefaces and asked me to select fonts and point sizes. Huh? In 1969 this was Greek to me. I looked at Jim for his opinion, but he refused to intervene. "You're the designer, Jane."

He challenged me by making me responsible for major decisions that could make or break the show. His generosity was monumental to me as an emerging artist and entrepreneur. His trust that I could deliver a superior product helped me respect myself as an artist.

❊   ❊   ❊

LESSON 67

A mastermind group can help you develop to the point where you can afford luxuries with or without a tax write-off.

For years I'd been trying to figure out how to go to a luxury spa and write off the trip as a business expense. Many business conferences are held at great locations, hotels, and resorts. Those business trips are fully deductible for the participants. Why couldn't I take an expensive trip to some luxurious locale and work on strategic planning with a group of advisors? My accountant informed me that as long as the trip was business-related—and could be documented as such—it would be an acceptable tax deduction. I decided that somehow, someday, I would figure out a way to go to a Golden Door or Canyon Ranch and get a tax write-off. Greed can work for you when you're an entrepreneur.

In the mid-1990s, I formed a support group for my business that is still going strong. I invited several of my entrepreneurial friends to my home for a brainstorming session. I wanted to assemble a mastermind group that would meet monthly *and* take an annual spa retreat for the purpose of professional development and business planning. Mastermind groups were mentioned on the audiotapes I listened to regularly. A group consists of hand-chosen business advisors from different industries who meet regularly to focus on one another's business.

Our group, nicknamed NYCONN for its members hailing from New York and Connecticut, has been meeting monthly ever since. We gather at one of our offices at the end of the workday and share a quick bite. Conversation over dinner is social. At 6:30 p.m., we begin going around the circle, focusing on each member's business for a specified amount of time.

The advantages of this association are profound. For one thing, once a month I know that I am accountable to these other women for what I want to accomplish. Our format requires each of us to set goals monthly.

At the beginning of the session, we each talk about the outcomes of the previous month's goals.

The second round is to focus on challenges—what's giving us difficulty in the workplace. I've used my focus time to try out a new speech or to ask for input on suggestions for a book I was writing. Others have discussed employee issues, burnout, and frustration over rejections.

The next and final round is to set goals for the following meeting. As the goal-setting monitor, I always force members to make sure their goals are realistic and specific. We also make sure that those goals require more effort than activities a member would accomplish anyway. Attending a monthly association meeting is not a goal, while traveling to the International Toy Fair in Nuremberg is.

In addition to having the opportunity to talk about my business with other professionals, I get to hear what's going on in other fields. I feel less isolated, get a larger worldview, and have my efforts validated by business owners I respect.

We've had several celebrations as goals are reached, including a dinner treat at a local restaurant when the owner of a gift business hired a new sales rep, and a gourmet meal when a member secured another backer for her organization.

The spa trip hasn't happened yet, although I can tell it's closer to reality. It's great to have a goal for us to work toward as a group. My dream was big, a tax-deductible spa vacation. The irony is that I achieved a truly bigger goal, an ongoing support system for my business that enabled the success to afford spas without a write-off.

※　※　※

LESSON 68
A fail-safe method to move toward a goal: promising a colleague you will accomplish a challenging task within a specified time.

In my first book, I wanted to illustrate the phenomena that occur with the aniline dyes I used to color my egg designs. Dye sequencing is a curious part of that craft adhering to idiosyncratic dictates rather than traditional color theory. I knew it would be informative and visually compelling for readers. Yet I couldn't discipline myself to sit down and figure out a way to treat this project in text and photos. I kept saving it for later, and the deadline for my book was rapidly approaching.

One afternoon I sat next to a talented florist at an Entrepreneurial Woman's Network event. The speaker's topic was committing yourself to a goal. She asked each of us to share an undertaking we had been putting off. My partner, the florist, had her own task she had been avoiding. I told her mine. We had taken the first step toward making our goals real.

On my way home, I stopped at the grocery store and picked up five dozen eggs. I was so charged with my mission I couldn't wait to get home. Once there, I started to work on dye-sequencing variables. I recorded the egg-dyeing process, noting each step along the way. Then I created a chart that identified how each of the colors was achieved, the amount of time the egg remained in each dye bath, and in what order the dyes were used. I needed motivation and accountability, and the florist's interest in my task and description of hers were enough to get me going. Years later, I still remember the power of that first experience in accountability. I knew someone out there was aware of my challenge. I felt encouraged to report back the results of my work, knowing that I would receive acknowledgment for working on it.

For the chart in my book, I ultimately dyed more than sixty eggs to demonstrate what happened with different dye combinations. Readers frequently compliment me on this section in my book. However, executing that job was more valuable to me than it was to them.

※ ※ ※

LESSON 69
Ask for informational support
and emotional support.

Growing up, I had the idea that I should never admit when I didn't know something. I interpreted this to mean that I should never ask questions. The overriding message was that I shouldn't appear stupid. So I took part only in things I was familiar with. Furthermore, I felt morally superior to anyone who had the stupidity to admit that he or she didn't know something. My disgust was further compounded when the offenders publicly asked for answers. How could they? One day I realized that those silly people who were asking all those dumb questions were getting a whole lot further ahead in life than I was. When I began changing my attitude, I was amazed that no one said I was stupid.

There were two sides of my problem. Not only did I hate to ask for help, but I had difficulty helping anyone. I believed that if I shared my knowledge, my information store would be diminished, so I shelled out facts like a miser giving alms. Most people are delighted when someone asks them for help. I also noticed how generous other people were when I called them for information. I began to notice how flattered I became when someone called to ask if a craft show was worth attending, what database program I used, or if I could recommend a bookkeeper. I marveled at their willingness to expose their vulnerability, their lack of know-how.

I had the opportunity to put asking for help to an extreme test. An executive outplacement company had invited me to speak to its candidates about entrepreneurship. I had a couple of months to prepare. I was looking forward to helping these ex-executives see the benefits of having their own enterprises. Two weeks before the engagement, I called several of them to ask about their expectations and needs. Although they had been corporate employees, many had acted like entrepreneurs as part of their jobs—managing acquisitions and mergers or heading up parts of the company as intrapreneurs. The talent I discovered in the audience intimidated me. Two days before the event, I wanted to drop out.

Because I'd learned to show up no matter what, I realized this wouldn't be an option. But what could I do? I asked for help. I called my friend Patty, who had arranged this speaking engagement. She told me, "Jane, I picked you because you have made a business out of something entirely unthinkable. Who else could tell these guys about being an entrepreneur?" I called my friend Steve, a business coach. "You're not going to tell them the 'how' or the 'what.' Your strength is in demonstrating the 'who' of entrepreneurship." In total, I called fourteen friends and colleagues. Each filled in a piece of why I had agreed to give the talk in the first place. I made the decision to show up.

When the candidates assembled that Thursday morning, we introduced ourselves. In the audience was a professor from a local college who taught entrepreneurship. "I'm here to keep you honest, Jane," he said with a smile and a wink. Now, I thought, I'm in deep trouble. But he supported everything I said, including my response to one earnest participant who asked if a start-up business owner should hire all the professionals he needed right away—lawyers, accountants, etc. "In my experience," I shared, "I hired as needed. When a legal issue arose, I found a lawyer."

The college professor nodded approvingly. The former executives loved my stories of tenacity and success, and they got my message: entrepreneurship is a satisfying lifestyle decision that has its trials and tribulations like any other form of business. Their smiles and relaxed postures showed me that they recognized and appreciated the joy I feel in my work.

That morning, my biggest achievement was walking through the door of the conference room to face my fear and deliver my message. The other reward came when one of the candidates came up to me afterward. He had been an executive with a major Wall Street banking firm. "I've always had a dream of becoming an artist," he said. "You have reawakened that possibility for me. Thank you." My willingness to set aside my false pride and ask for help was doubly rewarded that day.

※　※　※

LESSON 70
Articulating your plan to a sympathetic person makes it easier to begin doing it.

"If you don't hear from me within a half-hour, you may need to send an ambulance to my house." I was talking to my friend Pat because I needed some bolstering. I was planning to call the gift buyer at Neiman Marcus, and my heart was beating so fast it scared me. Having another soul out there who knew and cared about me and what I was about to do has been a godsend. Also, once I'd committed myself to make the move and told a sympathetic friend or colleague, there was no backing out.

Immediately after I hung up the phone with Pat, I dialed the Neiman Marcus headquarters in Dallas. I got the buyer's voice mail. What a relief! I'd followed through on my commitment without having to actually speak to the buyer. Voice mail let me hear the buyer's disembodied voice so I developed a mental image of her. I also learned when it would be convenient for me to try again. I was thrilled that I had taken this first step. I knew it would be much easier to call the next time. I had gotten my feet wet. Wading in up to my knees would be that much simpler. I called Pat back to share my excitement.

"Bookending" is a term I've borrowed from 12-step recovery programs. A book cannot stand upright easily. It needs support on each side from other books. Books are not unlike people. In recovery programs, you are encouraged to take risks with the aid of another concerned member of the organization. Bookending gives home office workers what the water cooler provides in corporations—a place to find support.

It works reciprocally, too. While it was helpful to know that I could call Pat and bookend my fears, it also helps when I'm the recipient of a call. One day Pat called me when she decided to master the electronic keyboard she had recently purchased: "I'm vowing to go through the instruction book page by page and not take any shortcuts." Pat said she'd spend the next two hours reading through the manual. She inspired me. I had recently purchased a digital camera I assumed I should know how to use. Her example motivated me to study the instruction pamphlet, a step I often skip. I was also honored that she trusted me enough to reveal that she, too, was mortal and did not know how to do everything perfectly the first time.

※   ※   ※

LESSON 71

Hiring a coach for a month or a year is a worthwhile investment.

On our Tuesday morning walks at Compo Beach in Westport, Connecticut, Alicia and I often talked about our families and our lives, but mostly we talked about our businesses. She owns a travel agency that provides customized tours. For weeks she kept referring to a woman called Valerie, who seemed to be important to her company. When I finally asked her who Valerie was, she said, "Valerie is a member of the International Coach Federation. She suggested that I add at least three clients to my roster this quarter as a way of increasing revenues without overselling my current clients. I've been cruising the Internet looking for organizations in New England that I haven't approached yet about my garden tours." I thought I could benefit from someone like Valerie.

I got to meet Valerie face to face at an Entrepreneurial Woman's Network event a few months later. This is important to note because even though I was intrigued and knew I could benefit from the help, it required seeing this service provider in the flesh before I would try her services. We made a phone appointment for a trial coaching session.

My way of doing business changed dramatically after I began working with Valerie, but I can't explain exactly what she does or how she does it. At first, I attempted to analyze her method, her questions, and her responses—for about five minutes. Then the process took over, and I became so engrossed in self-exploration that I forgot to pay attention to what Valerie was doing.

She guided me through the development of the Circle of Life collection—my "Dozen Eggs" in a glass carton. It was Valerie who cheered me on as my own enthusiasm dampened following disappointment after disappointment. She was there to listen, encourage, and nudge me forward. She also suggested that I record every step of the journey, because it would make a great speech or book one day.

In addition, when my enthusiasm flagged, Valerie asked me probing questions. She helped me uncover hidden feelings from my earliest childhood that had kept me emotionally handicapped and prevented me from moving forward. I used to think that maybe I was the only one who suffered from the bondage of early behavior patterns, until I read an article in the business section of the *New York Times* about two real estate moguls who were fighting over a piece of property. One of them bid a ridiculously high amount for a building simply because he didn't want the other guy to have it. Talk about childhood issues. Who doesn't need to examine his behavior?

Hiring a coach is a smart move for soul proprietors, executives, or anyone interested in moving forward in life. Part of Valerie's success as my coach was that she taught me to ask myself the kinds of questions she would pose. She empowered me to understand my motives and fears so that I could recognize and deal with them. Or reach out for help when I couldn't do it on my own.

※　※　※

LESSON 72
The success story of someone who has traveled the route before you can help you stay on course.

Charna Garber, the president of a luxury shoe manufacturing company, was the keynote speaker at my Entrepreneurial Woman's Network luncheon. She described her first trip to Italy to meet the foreman of the leather shop that would produce her company's shoes. It was not only her first time in that country, but also her first experience driving a car with a manual transmission. As she jerked back and forth along the highway on her way to meet a stranger in a strange land, she thought, "What am I doing here? What have I gotten myself into?"

It got worse. When she arrived at the factory, Tony, the foreman, was shocked that the new president of the shoe company was a woman. He turned his back on her, saying he wouldn't work with her. Because she didn't have any options other than getting back into the rental car, she stood up to him: "You at least have to give me a chance." He did. When she reported her story to us, their relationship was well into its second decade.

I was on my way to exhibit my work at a craft show in Boston one snowy Thursday morning in December. I had racks on top of my van and a carload of display pieces and merchandise. The snow was falling heavily. My car was swerving back and forth, and I wasn't sure where the thruway entrance was. Tears started streaming down my cheeks. All I wanted was to be home by a fire, snuggled up under a quilt with a good novel. But I didn't turn back. Instead, I thought of Charna Garber.

These are the moments when I use prayer. Otherwise, my head becomes filled with negative thoughts, and I do believe we bring into our lives what we think about. So I said the serenity prayer several times, and the moment passed. The show was a success, and the storm became a badge of honor in my entrepreneurial rucksack.

I realize that not everything is going to be easy. To achieve success, there will be uncomfortable, even scary moments. A friend once said in reference to raising our children that as long as the general direction is forward, it's good. I continue to move forward no matter what. Knowing that other women are ahead of me on the journey motivates my travels.

※   ※   ※

LESSON 73
Taking the steps to feel like a pro yields far more than a feeling.

Why would a Ph.D., associate professor, and author of three books choose to hire a coach? "Accountability" was Dr. Debbie Danowski's short answer to that question. "That and encouragement."

Debbie joined one of my coaching groups with the desire to feel more like a professional writer. She was already employed full time at a local university, where she had regular office hours, a set schedule, and a title. What she wanted was to create the same structure and atmosphere when she was wearing her writer's hat.

As I do for all of my clients, I simply posed the questions: "What would that look like? Who is Debbie the Professional Writer?" Debbie provided the answers from her own creativity and self-knowledge. She imagined that a Professional Writer would:

- Create a dedicated workspace.
- Write two hours per day three days per week.
- Develop a press kit filled with clips of her writing.

From there it was easy. Our meeting dates were already set, so she knew how long she had to accomplish her goals. The first month was devoted to clearing out a space for a home office and setting it up with a comfortable writing area. She also committed to writing at regular intervals.

The second month, Debbie worked on creating a one-sheet that would serve as a snapshot of her writing career. This document included her photo and bio, a list of her publications, bullet points enumerating her specific areas of expertise, and testimonials. It functioned as a visual résumé for her prospects. Plus, she continued writing regularly.

This preparation and dedication generated writing assignments, which Debbie used to fill a growing and increasingly prestigious press kit.

Knowing that she would be checking in with our group on a monthly basis kept Debbie on task. She also knew that her colleagues were equally invested in her success—as she was in theirs. The group took on an energy of its own that propelled the individual members beyond their own expectations.

Debbie's fourth book, *The Emotional Eater's Book of Inspiration*, came out in January of that year. At our final session, I asked her if she was feeling more like a pro. She looked at me with curiosity. She had come so far in her writing career that she had all but forgotten her original goal. When you are in the process of fulfilling your visions and desires, you stop looking over your shoulder at how others see you and start living your dreams.

※　※　※

LESSON 74
Stay productive, not busy, with the help of a V.A.

While meeting with a group of speaking peers several years ago, Lynne, one of the most successful participants, helped the rest of us understand what had been most beneficial in increasing her productivity. She said her V.A. took over the responsibility for setting up Lynne's online newsletter each week, allowing Lynne to focus more on developing speech content. The V.A. spent an hour weekly researching organizations for our friend to approach with her marketing message. Not only that, but the V.A. took all the registrations for upcoming workshops, again freeing Lynne for the more important work of networking and meeting with prospects.

Almost in unison, those of us hearing this asked, "What's a V.A.?"

"Oh. It stands for virtual assistant."

This relatively new industry offers off-site, independent, highly capable subcontractors who take over as much administrative and creative work as the business owner is willing to let go of. Letting go is the key phrase here, as so many of us have trouble delegating.

I hired my first V.A., Tonya, in 2004. It was a great relief. I distinctly remember the first month we worked together. I had signed on to retain Tonya's services for a minimum of ten hours per month. Remember that a virtual assistant is trained to do administrative tasks. These to-dos used to take me hours, such as setting up spreadsheets for classes or trying to get my Word document newsletter into HTML format for online distribution. I had delegated what felt like weeks' worth of work to Tonya. Halfway through the month, fearing that I would be well over the ten hours allotted and in hock for three times that, I called Tonya and asked where we stood in terms of hours. "You've used up two and a half hours so far," she said matter-of-factly. I was shocked, elated, and giddy, almost feeling that I had gotten away with something.

Tonya had saved me hours and hours of my time in exchange for work that was so simple for her it took her only minutes per task.

Needless to say, I got much more accomplished from that point, delegating virtually everything I could and holding onto only those items that required my unique talent.

Tonya, whom I never met, worked for me for several years. Eventually, one of Tonya's clients bought up all of her time, and I had to find a new V.A. to take over all that I had been delegating. Fortunately, I was introduced to Valerie, who has been working for me ever since, virtually. We have not met in person yet, but she is virtually one of the most important people in my company, in every sense of that word.

※　※　※

CHAPTER 8

Feed Your Golden Goose – Self-Care Matters

While it's a mother's job to be sure her offspring are well cared for, that role ends when the child reaches eighteen or twenty-one. But who takes over from there? I had hoped some magical fairy godmother would enlist for that position once I was on my own, but she never showed up. It took me years to realize that my personal happiness and care fell squarely on my shoulders. I would have designed it otherwise, but I'm no deity.

My business role model, Eileen Fisher, is known for contributing financially to the wellness regimen of each of her employees every year with a generous stipend for that purpose. Since I am my own boss, it is up to me to schedule, finance, and show up for my own rest and renewal.

This is joyful work. I make the time, pay for it, and show up happily to enjoy my meditation, relaxation, and pampering respites.

LESSON 75

Baby steps turn into giant leaps when you make a commitment to improve yourself a little bit each day.

Alan Weiss, author of *Million Dollar Consulting*, advocates a philosophy, the "1% Solution™," which challenges us to improve at a minimum rate of one percent a day. Weiss's "solution" has become a watchword for me. Thanks to him, I often tell myself, "You can do that better, one percent better." Sometimes this practice doesn't produce results immediately. At first, it hardly shows. And I resent this—when I work harder, I want to see fireworks.

I noticed this pattern as I was preparing a mailing for a client. Instead of including some information about a Web site she ought to look at, I attached a Post-it telling her simply that she ought to check it out, and I sealed the package. Then I had this feeling in my gut, always a signal that I was not comfortable with what I had just done. I examined the feeling and heard the voice beneath it say, "She's your client. Why don't you look up the site yourself and send her the information? Save her that step. Make yourself a resource for her. Go the extra one percent." I opened the package, did the research on the Web site, and sent her the information. As insignificant as this sounds, to me it was major. Once I've put something on the pile to go to the post office, I'm done with it. It's almost heresy to change that pattern. This time I chose to do it right, to do it better.

Two things happened. I discovered more about that particular site, which became valuable in my own work, and I became the kind of person who takes that extra step. As with any muscle, once I flexed it, it became easier to work it. I'm sure my client had no idea of the process I went through. She may or may not have benefited from the information I sent. But I benefited from my action by extending myself, by growing that one percent, and by becoming the kind of person who takes responsibility and initiative.

※　※　※

LESSON 76
Occasionally the planets may line up to force you to take time off.

"I can't reach any of my prospects on the phone, my assistant is away for a few days, and my Internet access is on the fritz. I don't seem to be getting anything done," I complained to a friend, hoping for a modicum of sympathy in return.

"Sounds like the universe wants you to take a vacation," she said with a smile.

How much more information did I need? Toughing out those dark periods by trying to accomplish something is often an exercise in frustration. I remember a woman I met at a networking luncheon who stood out because she was walking with a cane and had an impressive-looking bandage on her foot. I introduced myself and pointed to her injury. "It's nothing glamorous. I was walking down the driveway to pick up my mail and tripped on a pebble. I broke two bones in my foot. The funny thing is, for weeks before this happened I kept repeating to myself, 'I need a break. I need a break.' "

The more I learn how to read the "breaks" the universe sends me and respond to them by taking time off, the less likely I'll wind up frustrated or walking with a cane.

※　※　※

LESSON 77
Taking time for yourself enhances your ability and desire to achieve your calling.

"You want me to do what?" asked Dr. Maryanne Ducey in our second coaching call. It was a request I often make of my clients. But for this ultra-busy and committed chiropractor and community leader, it seemed out of the question. "Take a day off just for you," I challenged her.

Maryanne has a jampacked life. She maintains a full practice, manages a household, and cares for her Kerry blue terrier, too. How, she wondered, could she possibly take a day away for something as seemingly frivolous as time at the lake?

(N.B. If alarms are going off in your head—especially if they're saying, "I could *never* do that" —this lesson is definitely for you.)

During our first call, Maryanne talked about wanting to feel excited about her life again. She wanted her Wheel of Life (an assessment tool that allows the client to visualize where the gaps in her life are) in balance and to put away more money for herself. How would taking a day trip in any way impact these desires?

When she returned from her assigned recreational activity, she was bubbling over with enthusiasm. In our subsequent call, she was exploding with her newfound wisdom. "When I get time for myself," she proclaimed, "the energy from that yields three times my normal productivity."

I have seen this result many times. There's an inexplicable element here that gets lost in translation. I suspect there is some hormonal justification or quantum physics description, but Maryanne's testimonial said it better than all of that.

As our coaching relationship has continued, Maryanne, like my other clients, has achieved her desires: feeling excited about her life, balancing out the gaps on her Wheel of Life, and making more deposits into her accounts—both financial and spiritual.

Clients also notice that their life purposes become fulfilled. Taking care of ourselves first enables us to perform the greater work of changing people's lives through our work.

In Maryanne's case, by modeling what optimum health looks like, she uses all of herself. Her chiropractic expertise plus her vibrant, healthy presence transform those who come to her for healthier lives.

My "prescription" to all busy entrepreneurs: take time for yourself on a regular basis—and call me in the morning!

※　※　※

LESSON 78
Boundaries created with care and kindness are easier to enforce.

My good friend Jessica authored her first book in 2009. She took the risk of asking Anne Lamott, one of my all-time favorite writers, to provide a blurb for the book cover. The message she got back from Anne Lamott's agent was that Anne had declared a *blurbatorium*—a creative and less hurtful way of saying no to such requests.

I wasn't completely surprised by that response. I'd attended a talk by Anne at the 92nd Street Y in New York City when her book *Blue Shoe* came out. She declared onstage that night that she almost stopped writing books because of her dread of autographing them at readings and book signings. It was so painful to think of creative ways to inscribe books that she knew she had to say something rather than avoid publicity tours. Her solution was to announce her sentiment and offer only her signature—no additional message—which attendees willingly line up to receive. She is a role model for how to take care of yourself in spite of others' needs and projections. She gently and humorously tells the truth.

I love her power of example. What it demonstrates is that with creativity, grace, and humor, any one of us can steer clear of tasks that weigh us down and stay focused on the work we love and thrive on.

※　※　※

LESSON 79
Design your business to financially and mentally support your time off.

Augusts are all about doing things differently and taking time off from my business. Over the years, I've designed my schedule to produce income in ten months of the year, allowing for a summer break and a typically quiet December. I use the weeks in August primarily for vacation, but also to regroup for the fall programs. Because the holidays are usually slow for coaching, I use the latter part of December for business planning, goal setting, and end-of-year review.

In July I let my clients know that our next appointments will be in September, then make plans that will take me in other directions. A typical schedule for away-from-my-routine outings includes a family vacation to the Jersey Shore, attending a conference that's of interest to me personally, and offering my services at a coaching training session. The Coaches Training Institute, through which I am certified, offers opportunities to assist at its three-day courses in New York City. There I can immerse myself in the language of coaching, work with masters in the field, and meet dozens of colleagues at all stages of their coaching development.

Each of these accomplishes, in its own way, the same outcomes that are the hallmarks of what a vacation represents for this woman business owner: time away from my everyday activities, being with people I enjoy, meeting new people, and trying new things. Also, it is critically important to get out of my environment to change my perspective, which always happens as a direct result of not being home in my office.

For some people, this entails travel to exotic places. For me, changing my routine and becoming completely absorbed in something else feels right. When I'm back at my desk, I feel invigorated and refreshed to do what I do the rest of the year.

I can't wait to talk to my clients again. I look forward to the networking events on my calendar. I'm excited to see my colleagues who have been off doing wonderful things as well.

✳ ✳ ✳

LESSON 80
Doing *nothing* by appointment is essential and energizing.

One assignment I had during my coaching certification program was to sit for one hour and do nothing. I chose to bring my collapsible chair to Compo Beach on Long Island Sound for this hour of nothingness. It was chilly, so I had a blanket wrapped over my body. The tide was low and coming in.

Within a few minutes of disorientation—how does one do nothing?—I began to observe what was going on in the nothingness of sitting. I started watching the gulls. One would swoop down, pick up a clamshell in its beak, fly up, and drop it to the ground. When it broke open, the bird would swallow the contents—mission accomplished.

I noticed that the activity would be repeated two or three times if the shell wasn't immediately compliant. The bird simply swooped down again, retrieved the same shell, flew up, and dropped it again. After a couple of tries without success, it moved on to another shell. It was a force of nature. No judgment. Just . . . NEXT. Even in that time of doing nothing, I noticed my brain assessing, judging, making sense out of what was in front of me. I applied it to myself and my clients. How refreshing, natural, and healthy to observe what's working, what feeds you, and when to let go. There's always a NEXT. Keep moving. Keep doing what you do. And when the tide flows in, move on to the next activity for the day.

The outcome of that assignment for me was connecting with nature, giving my mind a healthy distraction, and not having any responsibility for what was happening in front of me. I left the beach with a renewed sense of energy and optimism.

※　※　※

CHAPTER 9

Catch the Curve Balls – Grow and Adjust Along the Way

I once served on a panel of entrepreneurs at Quinnipiac College in Hamden, Connecticut. During the Q & A period following our presentations, an aspiring business owner student asked optimistically, "When do you get to put your feet up on your desk, lean back, and enjoy the ride?"

We panelists glanced back and forth at one another as if to reinforce our own experience that this, in fact, never happens. As business owners we are constantly finding new challenges and markets to conquer. When it starts to get easy, it gets boring. We're on to the next mountain.

Which doesn't make the hurdles any easier to leap or the delight in our war stories any less satisfying. It is the cumulative and transformative effect of hurdling those obstacles that makes our paths compelling. If we already knew all the answers and could solve all the problems, we entrepreneurial types would fold up our tents and go home.

Bring it on! But, here, let me show you my scars.

LESSON 81

There are always days that are slated for growth or learning. Stay with them and don't get upset.

Pedro Boregaard, a jeweler I know, described a situation I am familiar with. He had worked on a pin for days, and the more he worked on it, the more he knew it wasn't the way he wanted it. He completed the brooch but knew that it still wasn't right. He moved on. The next dozen or so pieces were effortless and perfect. I find that if I stay with a difficult process, there is a lesson to be learned.

For example, a woman commissioned me to make an egg celebrating the iron gates at Brown University that were opened only two times a year, at convocation and graduation. She wanted it as a gift for her daughter who was graduating from Brown.

I had to paint that majestic image on an eggshell. I worked out a design, dyed the egg, and proceeded to lay it out. Halfway through the process, I was fairly certain that the black dye was not dark enough. But I continued anyway because I wanted to see if I could get away with it and if the rest of the design would work. When I completed the egg and removed the wax to reveal the colors beneath, my heart sank a little. It was just OK. It wasn't great. The gates were closer to gray than black and didn't seem to convey enough power. A friend who taught art stopped by the next day, and I asked his opinion, hoping that since he didn't know what I was striving for, the egg would still appeal to him. I really didn't want to do it over. His words were nonjudgmental but final: "My eye wants to see more contrast."

I started over, making sure this time that the bath of black dye had saturated the egg before I proceeded. That second attempt came out perfectly. I had achieved my original goal. The customer called me as soon as the egg arrived to thank me profusely.

I've often looked for the shortcut, but sometimes there isn't one. It's always better to push for the correct solution.

I found a poem that describes the process perfectly.

It is a pleasure
When, after a hundred days
Of twisting my words
Without success suddenly
A poem turns out nicely

It is a pleasure
When spreading out some paper
I take a brush in hand
And write far more skillfully
Than I could have expected

Haiku by Tachibana Akemi (1812-1868) — Translated by Donald Keene

※   ※   ※

LESSON 82

It's important to know when to discard something you already have for the promise of something better to come.

For years I ran a successful business out of a makeshift studio in our converted family room. Orders came in. I decorated eggs at a decent pace. It was all working well. But I kept tripping over the wires that connected the new computer and printer. The telephone was on the opposite side of the room from my workspace. The file cabinets jutted out of the wall, blocking the path from my design area to my egg-decorating area. Every time I made a mental note that these small inconveniences should be improved, I resisted taking any action.

However, once I realized that a renovated studio would make an enormous difference in my production and self-image, I moved forward and found an architectural designer to map out all the areas I envisioned. Just imagining a dedicated area for dealing with epoxy and another area to be used solely for shipping lightened my heart. Not only would I be more efficient, but also my spirit would be uplifted. My creativity, enthusiasm, and output would increase.

What I didn't anticipate was the sheer drudgery of getting through the renovation. "What was I thinking?" I asked my husband as we watched the movers pack up every piece of equipment and furniture in my studio and carry it into our living room, where I was going to set up shop in the interim—hopefully for only thirty days.

I was miserable. The light in the living room was dreadful. Interruptions were constant. Our kids used the room to watch TV, talk on the phone, and relax. Close quarters without a private sanctuary strained relations between my family and me.

It's always darkest before the dawn. Just when I thought I couldn't stand it a moment longer, the renovation was completed and I began moving my equipment back into my studio and out of the family's space. A week later, the room was painted, the floor tiles were laid, and I had a magnificent space to work. The raw emotions of the month before were transformed from anger to deeper intimacy. We had survived the renovation.

Going into the hell of remodeling, I knew I would be rewarded if I could just be patient and persevere. By resisting the temptation to settle for satisfactory short-term rewards, I ended up with the greater long-term benefits. I am convinced that entrepreneurs can measure their success by their willingness to forgo immediate results for the promise of greater, more lasting gains.

※   ※   ※

LESSON 83
Consider yourself lucky if there are only minor irritations in your day.

It takes a lot to move me out of my home office. I dislike leaving it to run errands. I would prefer to hire someone to do them for me, but there are never enough to justify it.

After focusing closely on a project for a few hours, I usually take a break midmorning and do the errands with my mail run. One day I decided to start out early in order to wrap up some particularly annoying minor tasks—banking, a pickup at the printer two towns away, and a purchase at the office supply store. The store and my printer would be open by 7 a.m., so I figured I would start with them and end up at the bank, where the drive-through window opened at 8:30 a.m.

Into the life of any entrepreneur, a little rain must fall. Considering the possibilities, this catalog of a morning's events seems minor, but to the person involved it can be major, even overwhelming. Here's the scenario: I leave my house at 7:45 a.m., giving myself forty-five minutes to accomplish two tasks before I land at the bank window in time for the 8:30 a.m. opening.

Strategically I drive to my farthest destination first to pick up a job at the printer. I pull up at the building and know at once that the hand-lettered sign stuck with tape on the door is not a message I want to read. "Back in one hour." I have a system. I always keep a "rip and read" folder of magazine articles and downloaded printouts in my car or in my bag that I can pull out anytime I find myself in a holding pattern. Doctors' offices, bank lines, and airports drive me crazy if I don't have something to do to pass the time. This particular morning, I don't have my folder with me. To sit there stewing is not an option. I leave in a huff.

Next on my list is the office supply store, where I need a special mailing label for a marketing piece I'm going to send out. To make my mailings as personal as possible, I like to use transparent labels. They give the illusion that the address is printed right on the envelope. The office supply store is out of the transparent labels. I am now two for two in the failure column.

Sometimes I begin to wallow in self-pity. "Why is this happening to me? I'm cursed. Poor me." With a glimmer of hope, I think, "At least I'll be first in line at the bank." I am pleased to see there's no line of cars, but when I drive up, I understand why. There's a note announcing the hydraulic function at the drive-through window is broken. And the bank won't open its doors until 9 a.m.

Inevitably, after moaning and groaning about the unfairness of life and my burdens, I will encounter someone far less fortunate than me—a person with a visible handicap that won't be better tomorrow. And I straighten up and stop griping. Instead I take the time to list the things I am grateful for. It helps remind me how lucky I really am.

❊   ❊   ❊

LESSON 84

As you work, continually evaluate the next thing you have to do in order to succeed.

Particularly because I have a home office, I frequently have to take care of the daily trivia, along with my work. Sometimes I feel overwhelmed, and that's when I know it's time to evaluate the importance of any task. Here's an example. Time savers hold a special place in my heart. When I am introduced to a product that will save me precious minutes or even seconds, I consider it. The first time I saw a shampoo dispenser attached to the tiled wall of a hotel bathroom, I thought, "What a great idea! No more taking the caps off and putting them on." Shortly after that, I saw the same item advertised in a catalog. I joyously ordered it, knowing the gadget would give me even more time to enjoy the steaming hot water and less time fiddling with bottles and jars. I felt smug. I had discovered a better mousetrap.

That was short-lived. Within days, the dispenser became clogged and stopped working. I called customer service at the catalog company. "We'll be happy to refund your money on that product. But we've discontinued our relationship with the vendor and can't contact them. If you like, you can take it up with them directly." Well, I really liked the idea of the dispenser and had enjoyed using it. I made an attempt, got a recording, waited for a call back, and tried once more. When I saw the "call again" on my to-do list a week later, I thought to myself, "How important is this right now? Not at all." I postponed the task. When that date arrived, I still didn't want to spend the time it would take to get the replacement dispenser or parts. So I crossed it off my list and let it go.

Now, let's translate this experience to work.

One morning I addressed an audience of realtors. The organizer was very enthusiastic about my talk and wanted me to offer more courses to his company. He sent me a Web site link where I could apply for certification so that future attendees could receive official credit for my teaching. While I might have gotten more speaking opportunities from this arrangement, I had to ask myself an important question: Is this what I really want? Where would it lead? Is this a market I want to pursue?

My gut was my guide. I said, "Thanks, but no," and moved on.

※   ※   ※

LESSON 85
Understand that getting from inspiration to completion is a complex journey with thrills and disasters guaranteed along the way.

"Hello, my name is Steve Jobs," the voice on the phone said. "I'd like to buy some of your eggs." If I got that call today, my heart would start pounding a mile a minute. I would visualize a skyrocketing bank account and start speculating how I could incorporate his name in future ads. But that call came in 1991, before I owned a Macintosh computer or had even heard of Steve Jobs.

He discovered my eggs when they appeared on the cover of the Flax Art & Design catalog that was mailed to 1.2 million people in the United States. I had won a contest sponsored by Flax. It all started on a hot, sticky summer day when my assistant, Jodi Fisher, handed me a mail-order catalog. The cover caught my eye. It featured a drawing of a white Holstein cow with an abstract-looking black mark covering its torso. On closer examination, it turned out to be the Flax logo—the letter "F." Jodi told me the catalog company was sponsoring a contest for a cover design incorporating the letter "F" and suggested that we enter.

It was one of those great ideas that inspire an immediate rush of brainstorming and enthusiasm, followed by hours and weeks of hard work, second-guessing, and self-criticism. Jodi drew up a sketch that would have been brilliant if we could have produced it. We simply couldn't get the concept to work. It was aggravating and disappointing to spend all that time, energy, and resources and get nowhere. It's also not unusual.

We loved the idea of integrating the "F" into an intricate egg pattern. We still wanted to enter the contest. Out of frustration and because of the upcoming deadline, I came up with a simple yet elegant solution: row after row of my quilt-design eggs, with one featuring the "F" in black and white within the quilt pattern. My good friend Carmine

Picarello photographed it, and we mailed the entry in just before the deadline. Three months later, we learned we had won first prize.

Staying with your inspiration from inception through completion is always more challenging than you can imagine, but the rewards are marvelous.

※   ※   ※

LESSON 86

Pursue your goals systematically. You will get where you want to go, but not necessarily the way you planned.

I joined the National Speakers Association and was told that Marcie, a mentor for beginners in the field, was outstanding for her knowledge of both the professional speakers marketplace and the entrepreneurial marketplace. I drove five hours twice a month for these sessions—once to meet with my class with Marcie and a second time to meet with the chapter as a whole to test our new skills.

Marcie's challenge was to help us find our way in the world of professional speakers. Determining target audiences was a major challenge, then developing marketing materials for those audiences. I wanted to target the education market with my topic: "Turning Your Passion Into a Business."

Every month we would bring in our latest marketing materials for feedback and suggestions. I brought along a sample letter that my graphic designer had formatted. My letter gave my qualifications and the topics I was qualified to talk about. It was addressed to the fine arts department chairs at liberal arts colleges. I offered to inspire—for a fee—students who were considering turning their talents into businesses, as I had. The professors were my target audience.

Marcie and the group liked what I'd written and my promotional kit containing press clippings, testimonials as to my competence, and my bio.

I sent my letter and press kit to thirty colleges, and even though Marcie and my group loved my packet, it turned out to be a dud. I received one polite rejection, while the other twenty-nine chairs ignored my phone calls. It took months to pursue this lead, and I got nowhere. But my enthusiasm for marketing and the quality of my materials had caught Marcie's eye. When a colleague asked if she knew someone who could conduct marketing seminars, she suggested me, and I got the interview.

I had lunch with Nancy Michaels, the principal of Impression Impact, a company that provided seminars for major corporations. She hired me to conduct a marketing seminar, "How to Be a Big Fish in Any Pond," at the Staples store in Kalispell, Montana. For several years, I happily delivered programs for Nancy's company all over the United States.

※　※　※

LESSON 87
Enjoy the ride, but don't let the ride drive you.

In the early 1980s, I knew I had made it when the phone rang in my studio and it was the White House. I was sure I was on the road to fame and fortune. I was invited to decorate an Easter egg for the annual Easter Egg Roll the following spring. What more could anyone ask? This news was carried in the local papers and has followed me since. It was a boon to my career and improved my credibility. But it was not the be-all and end-all.

Have you heard of the song *Big Nuthin'* by The Roches? The sisters who sang this song had been invited to perform on Johnny Carson's *Tonight Show*. It was the biggest break any entertainer could dream of. The day came, they appeared, and nothing happened. No ringing phones, no multi-record contracts or million-dollar signings. They wrote *Big Nuthin'* as a response to their disappointment. My friend Cookie, a successful children's book illustrator, had the same letdown. Her artwork appeared on a *New Yorker* magazine cover but failed to ring any bells.

I've had many such disappointments. In fact, there is a direct correlation between my expectations and what happened. The bigger the expectation, the bigger the letdown. There was a two-page spread in a glossy magazine that I was sure would bring me orders and fans by the hordes. I received one order. Another national magazine placed a beautifully done article about me in its January issue. It arrived in households about a week or two before Christmas, when reading magazines is a low priority, and few sales resulted.

On the other hand, when I do have a big hit, a funny thing begins to happen. After a four-page spread in the April 1990 issue of *Country Home* appeared, mail started to pour in and the orders flowed. It was exhilarating. For a while there, I felt as though I was the center of the universe. Sometimes, and I hesitate to say this, it almost feels like too much attention, like I wanted to fade back into a little obscurity.

When I got married, it felt as though the whole world was focused on me. My picture was in the paper. I felt celebrated, but at some point I also felt a certain lack of privacy and freedom. People called fairly regularly to ask about my wedding plans, then how the wedding was, and then how the marriage was.

Not too long afterward, I became pregnant and again felt like the sun in my universe. "Did you have the baby yet?" "Oh, you had the baby!" "How was the delivery?" Then came loads of gifts, correspondence, and visits by friends and family. I wondered if it would ever end. And then, it did. Daily life took over, and I wondered where all those people went. While I savored the privacy, a part of me felt the absence of all that attention.

While the White House opportunity and early press came out of the blue, I now choose to create those hits. This is where balance comes in. It's exciting for a business owner to be featured in any capacity—winning an award, being profiled in the newspaper, or appearing on TV. People are thrilled for you. But after a while, it becomes somewhat ordinary. The first time I appeared in the newspaper, a dozen or more people sent me clips. Now, after years of publicity, barely anyone takes the time. The message is clear. Enjoy the attention while you get it, but understand that it is fleeting. You also need a postpartum plan to keep your spirit and momentum alive.

※　※　※

LESSON 88

A sense of humor is helpful in learning humility.

An oversized ego has occasionally been an issue for me. For years I felt that I shouldn't have to work so hard, market so much, or donate any of my goods or services to charity. I grew up with a sense of entitlement that somehow, some way, I wasn't meant to get my hands dirty and that my reputation trumped humility. Bad lesson. Bad message.

Several weeks after a wonderful half-page write-up about me in the *New York Times*, a woman who saw it called to order my book. I asked how she had heard about the *Times* piece. Had some friend who had seen the article called to share her passion for Ukrainian eggs? No. She explained that a neighbor had given her old newspapers to line the bottom of the cages she used in her kennel service. She happened to open the section of the *Times* that contained the article about me, and that caught her eye. "I actually prefer getting the *Wall Street Journal*," she said, "because the paper they use is more absorbent."

※　※　※

LESSON 89
There will be things you don't even know you don't know until they come up.

The longer I'm in business, the more I know how much I don't know. And sometimes, I discover I don't know how much I don't know. I couldn't even have dreamed up the following experience. I did my first wholesale show one cold February weekend and took thousands of dollars' worth of orders for eggshell jewelry. When I returned to my studio, I figured out a production schedule and then called my supplier. I said I would need twenty dozen duck eggshells as soon as possible. There was silence at the other end. As gently as possible, my supplier informed me that the ducks wouldn't be laying eggs again until April. Could I place the order then? Accounting for Mother Nature had never occurred to me. I needed to go back to my customers and explain the situation. I did lose several sales, but most of the people told me they would wait.

It's not just the little guys who endure these lessons. I heard someone describe a corporate blunder. An American doll manufacturer she worked for had decided the company should design dolls specifically for the Europeans, since they were avid doll collectors. The dolls were magnificent, exquisitely dressed and coiffed. But there was one oversight: size. Most European houses are much smaller than American houses. The dolls were too large for the shelves in European houses. They had to be completely reworked at a cost of millions in time, research, and materials.

※   ※   ※

LESSON 90
Learn from each experience –
positive or negative – and move forward.

"Entrepreneurs fail their way to success," said Austin Pryor, a coun-selor with the Service Corps of Retired Executives (SCORE). I wouldn't have wanted to hear that at the beginning of my career, but as a seasoned pro, I can smile at its truthfulness. Yes, taking a business from start-up to ultimate success is not a straight path. There are twists and turns along the way, advances and retreats, and sometimes near disasters. While I've steered clear of any real disasters, I have taken a number of detours that set me back in my momentum. It's important to kiss the frog and hop on, to learn from each experience and move forward.

I sat next to Gigi Goldman at a networking event one afternoon. We established immediate rapport as we talked about my skills and hers and began to get very excited about the possibility of working together on a project. Gigi imported picture frames from overseas. She hired me to create design motifs for them and wanted to come up with a possible line to work on together.

We had several meetings to discuss themes, materials, and direction for the line. I created sketches, drawings, and finished paintings of the frame patterns. We met with a marketing person to help us position the line in the marketplace. I enjoyed every aspect of the relationship, as well as the work I was creating.

The glitch came when the factory overseas was unable to reproduce the colors in the designs I painted. Rather than working with porcelain, which has its own integrity, the factory was using a less expensive ce-ramic mold. The quality of the finished product was below the standards that both Gigi and I expected. Ultimately, after we both spent hundreds of hours and thousands of dollars on the project, Gigi decided to pull the plug.

I have experienced several dead ends like this in my business. You could call them failures, but along the way they taught me what I can't do and what I'm not good at. They also have shown me which dream I need to discard and which dream I need to continue dreaming. The frame project with Gigi taught me that I love collaborating. I love the synergy of working with another creative individual. I learned that it is difficult, if not impossible, to foresee what a foreign studio would do with the samples I sent. I learned that I prefer to have complete control over the end product.

I spent three years trying to become the next Laura Ashley, but time after time I received messages from the commercial world on the outside, and from my heart and brain on the inside, telling me that this was not my ultimate calling. Eventually I hopped off the design path and leapt on the professional speaking and coaching route and never looked back.

※   ※   ※

LESSON 91

What at first seems to be a humorous coincidence can be interpreted as a sign from the universe.

For years my universe revolved around me. I was the cause of rain at Shea Stadium when my husband had tickets to see the Mets. My harsh words to my daughter caused her best friend not to invite her to sleep over. I was responsible for everyone and everything. When I finally learned that I wasn't, it was an enormous relief. And I began to think that coincidences might possibly be the work of my higher power.

There was one coincidence that made me laugh out loud. I have become conscientious about writing down every bit of money coming in and going out both for my personal and for my business accounts. It's sometimes a nuisance. What I've learned, however, is that attention to detail gets the rewards, so I faithfully record every cent that crosses my path. I received a $50 gift certificate to a large bookstore, spent $40 of it in one shopping expedition, and was given a credit memo for $10. In the car, I began puzzling over how to record that debit and credit. It began to feel like too much work.

I rationalized that I shouldn't have to record the money from the gift at all. I deliberated some more. I became lost while I was doing all this reflecting. Then, as if from the beyond, Gary Puckett and The Union Gap's song playing on my car radio floated into my consciousness. "Woman, oh woman, have you got cheating on your mind?"

※　※　※

LESSON 92

When you acknowledge that your childhood feelings are interfering with your business relationships, you can move on.

For one full year, I pursued an industry I desperately wanted to buy my seminars—the egg producers of this country. It was an extensive campaign that included marketing materials, letters, phone calls, e-mails, and meetings. Finally, thirteen months after my introduction to Christine Bushway, the industry's marketing and promotions consultant, I was hired to conduct an egg-decorating workshop at a national meeting in California.

It was exhilarating. The workshop was a huge success. The group, made up of all the wives of the egg producers, loved having a session that wasn't about omelets or soufflés—the usual fare at these events. In addition, I sold egg-decorating kits, copies of my book, eggshell jewelry, and handmade ornaments. It was the perfect marketplace for me.

During the cocktail hour before the banquet, several women made a point of introducing me to their husbands and praising my program. I felt like their darling. I imagined I'd be on their roster as long as I liked. I thought I had it made. I looked forward to being hired to give workshops all over the United States. Not so. When a week passed and I hadn't heard from anyone, I thought maybe they were just planning a more thorough itinerary for me. I continued to keep in touch with Christine. She had heard the good reports and was eager to help keep the ball rolling. A month went by. Then two months. No bookings.

I was working with a business coach during this process. I gave her weekly updates. She noticed my flagging enthusiasm. After six months of phone calls and e-mails, I was ready to give up. When my coach asked what was happening with the egg people, I barked at her, "Forget it! If they're not dying to have me come back, I'm not going to keep pursuing it."

She adjusted her coaching hat. "Jane," she prodded, "tell me again how you felt during that presentation last October." I brightened at the memory. "It was one of the most rewarding days of my life. I loved doing it, and they seemed to love me. It was fun, lucrative, and just about the best thing I'd ever been involved in."

"Can you take a moment and think about what is happening to your enthusiasm?" Fortunately, I am always interested in why I behave the way I do. I'm not always comfortable with what I uncover, but I'm usually willing to have a look. "I hate the fact that they haven't pursued me. I'm disappointed and hurt. I want to walk away from them, so they don't have a chance to walk away from me."

It was an abandonment issue dating back to early childhood. It had nothing to do with the business I was running. I continued to pursue the egg people and presented several more times after overcoming that bout of ego inflation.

※　※　※

LESSON 93
Seeing a friend transformed by illness alters your definition of what a challenge is.

It was an early March morning when I drove to the rehabilitation center to see my friend Milles, who had had a brainstem stroke. Her family said she was recovering well and in good spirits. I had received a picture postcard of her sitting in a garden, and the mailing appeared to be in her handwriting.

The door to her room was slightly ajar, so I tapped lightly and entered. I was unprepared for what I saw next. She was strapped in a wheelchair, one eye turned in my direction, the other unfocused in another direction. The top of her warm-up suit was covered with food stains.

When she spoke to me, it was difficult to understand what she was saying. She had to repeat each word over and over until I could decipher it. Her mind was still brilliant, but her ability to communicate was severely impaired. It was agonizing for her and frustrating for both of us.

Her son Brennan arrived awhile later and gave me a full history of her recovery. She had been unable to speak at all immediately following the stroke. With frequent therapy and enormous persistence, she had worked up to the level I saw that day. Forming words took major effort—getting sufficient breath to pass over her vocal cords was a daily challenge. After an hour or two, I left, humbled by the vicissitudes of life and their effects on my friend.

Some time after my visit with Milles, I picked up an issue of *People* that gave a full report on Christopher Reeve's recent appearance at the Academy Awards show. It was his first appearance in public since the accident ten months before that had destroyed his spinal cord. The article described a spasm Reeve had suffered right before he was wheeled in front of the TV cameras. His entire body involuntarily had folded in half. He had to be physically pried back into a seated position to face the public.

I wondered what I could learn from both of these people without diminishing the awful thing that had happened to them. Why did they both cross my path in so brief a time? Two thoughts immediately came to mind. I realized that there is a great deal I take for granted in my daily life. Being able to breathe easily and form words clearly is not something I thank the universe for on a daily basis. Being able to move my body each day never seemed like a gift.

I also realized how often I paralyze myself in my work. Given the ability to speak, to think, and to act, I will still choose not to make the effort. At the time, I was working as a textile designer. As a result of my new realization of how lucky I was, and how simple the challenges facing me were compared with those of Milles and Christopher Reeve, I decided to go to New York to walk through the Decoration and Design Building. I had my portfolio with me and offered to show it to the art director of a well-known carpet manufacturer. I had dreamed about designing for a company like his but never had the courage to make the call.

He warned me before he took my portfolio: "If you design florals, we've got all we need." I answered, "My designs are mostly geometrics." After thumbing through my prints, he looked up and said, "These are exactly what we've been looking for." That immediate reinforcement of a new behavior became a touchstone I referred to whenever I found myself stalled. When I remember Milles and Christopher Reeve, I am encouraged to fully utilize my God-given gifts each day.

※　※　※

LESSON 94

Give the universe the opportunity to answer your prayers by being specific and asking for more than you can imagine.

When Jack Canfield, author of *The Success Principles*, teaches us how to write an affirmation, he's specific. It needs to be in the present tense, positive, brief, plus several other attributes, and ending with the phrase "or something better." The implication is that our dreams may be less grand than what the universe has in mind for us.

When co-leading a coaching program with my partner Brad Isaacs, I had reserved an elegant space at a nearby library for the event. Due to smaller than anticipated enrollment, we didn't need as large (or expensive) a space. I let go of the reservation, then started to seek a new room for our group. I kept coming up empty.

I allowed myself a moment of panic. "Oh, no! I'll *never* find a space. This is a disaster. I'm a failure." That lasted thirty seconds. Then I moved into action, which is always the secret weapon. I phoned the library to see if any other room existed or if we might negotiate. I left a voice mail. Then, I quickly scanned my brain for people in the area who might point me in another direction.

I called a former client and colleague who lives less than half a mile from that library. She knew the town well. Might she recommend a location for me?

"Have it here, at my house. I'll be away for the weekend. Come and get the key."

This woman is an award-winning interior designer. Her house is nothing short of spectacular. The room we got to use overlooks an impeccably landscaped backyard. It surpassed all my criteria for a functional space to lead a group—comfortable, serene, generous in size and feeling.

Allowing these miracles into my life didn't happen overnight. I've been practicing meditation, prayer, and affirmations and attending fellowship meetings for years. These have opened my eyes to seeing all the "something better" miracles that occur.

※　※　※

LESSON 95
Be alert for opportunities that come disguised as disappointments.

There's a familiar refrain out there. It goes something like this: "Since I never heard back from 'x' prospect, I decided to enroll in a course I'd been thinking of taking. I really got a lot out of it and am moving forward in this new direction." Substitute any opportunity that pops into your life or notice when a door you wanted to have opened doesn't. What are the alternatives?

As a baby boomer high school senior in the largest demographic to enter college, I was wait-listed at my first choice, Mount Holyoke College, and accepted at my safety school, George Washington University. Mount Holyoke had instituted a February Freshman program, allowing wait-listed students the opportunity to enter college in the winter, when early-graduating seniors would vacate rooms. I accepted that offer and attended GW for one semester.

Since I wasn't permitted to enroll in GW's freshman English course, (MHC wanted to be sure I took its), I had to substitute something from another discipline. I chose a life drawing course. Mount Holyoke's general education requirements included studies in the arts, so I knew the credits would transfer.

I hadn't been "allowed" to take art since eighth grade, when it had been part of the curriculum. It wasn't on the academic track at my high school, so I never signed up for classes there. When I *had* to substitute a course at GW, I enrolled in a nine-hour life drawing course—three three-hour sessions per week.

I never looked back. When I arrived at MHC, I continued taking art *and* theater courses, which became my split major. This uniquely qualified me for my first teaching job when I answered an ad for a stage-craft teacher in the art department at Westhill High School in Stamford, Connecticut. Thirty years in my own art business began shortly after my two-year stint at Westhill, where I was introduced to the art of Ukrainian Easter eggs.

Had I gotten into Mount Holyoke along with the rest of my class, would I have fallen in love with art the way I did during that intensive drawing class at GW? Who can say? What I thought was the worst luck at the time, not immediately getting into the college of my choice, turned into finding my life's work.

Life throws a lot of curves. We are constantly given choices as to what to do with opportunities or the seeming lack thereof. I'm convinced that following your passion and listening to your inner wisdom are the path to happiness. It may be a bumpy ride, but the direction is clear.

※   ※   ※

CHAPTER 10

Claim the Prize –
Enjoy the Rewards of
Soul Proprietorship

There's a skill in coaching called "MetaView," in which the coach instructs the client to imagine he or she is in a helicopter viewing the scene from 500 feet above. What does it look like from there? This allows the client a fresh perspective from that vantage point and always creates a shift in how the current issue is perceived.

While there have been untold challenges, hardships, and defeats throughout my career along with the victories and joy, when I get into that helicopter and look at the life I've created, I can't imagine doing anything else. I see a woman who has enormous freedom, who is involved with the most wonderful clients and associates, and who has created a rewarding world of her own design.

The essential ingredient in all of this is taking the time to notice, to bear witness to your own creation.

LESSON 96
When you show up and do the footwork, the universe clears a path for you.

When inspiration strikes, I make a commitment to a specific date, like "research entrepreneurial associations at the library" or "call the CEO of XYZ Corporation." It's painless to write the action on a calendar. That's why I do it first—to ease my way into the harder part.

The challenge comes when that day arrives and my assignment is due. I had promised myself to make travel arrangements to attend a valuable workshop in San Francisco. I shuddered. I had to decide exactly what time I needed to leave to fly to the West Coast and come back home. It also meant spending a significant amount of money. That doesn't sound so hard to do, but it's a lot harder than curling up on my comfy sofa with a good book.

Once I begin working through the stages to achieve a goal, invariably the universe steps in to help. That sustains me through the process. Before I called United Airlines, I checked to see how much frequent flier mileage I had earned. I had enough for a free domestic flight on United. The agent on the phone told me I had 10,000 more miles than I thought, leaving me only 105 miles shy of an upgrade to business class. No problem—he offered to credit me with those miles and debit them next time I flew United.

Goethe described this experience in this quotation I have hanging about my desk: "That the moment one definitely commits oneself then Providence moves, too." I find myself taking on bigger and bigger challenges just to see what cool surprises the universe will move my way.

※　※　※

LESSON 97

The more ambitious the vision, the more arduous the journey. The harder the journey, the bigger the thrill when it is completed.

In my goal-setting workshops, I use "singing arias at the Metropolitan Opera House" as an example of an unattainable goal because I am tone-deaf. But when Faith Ringgold said I should sell my eggs only by the dozen and in a glass egg carton, I knew her idea was not only a million-dollar concept but also achievable. Thrilling *and* possible.

For me, a good goal gives me a tingly feeling in my gut, as inspiration rushes into my brain. That feeling says, "This could be yours, Jane." What remains after that initial burst of enthusiasm and delight is the achievable portion, also known as hard work. Conceivable is the fun part; achievable tells the story behind success.

"What the mind can conceive and believe, it can achieve," Earl Nightingale said. His album *The Strangest Secret* was the first spoken-word recording to earn a gold record for selling a million copies. Its message: We become what we think about.

More than a year had passed since I'd met Faith Ringgold and taken her suggestion to heart. I then took one step every week to move the project forward, sometimes devoting each of those days to design patterns or research manufacturing options. When the owner of Artoria saw my painted eggs in the glass carton, she exclaimed, "Outrageous!" I knew I had finished the long trek. I had heard what Faith Ringgold had to say, recognized its importance, researched the production of the glass carton until I was exhausted, designed the eggs, packed up the shipping container carrying the eggs in a glass carton, and sent it to Artoria. I felt the thrill of success, not only in the final product but also in the realization I had done the work. I had come through on my dream.

Visions come to all of us. Achievement is seeing the vision become reality.

※　※　※

LESSON 98
What you do for pleasure is your passion.

How do you know if something is your passion? When I got into the car one day, I was in the middle of an audiocassette of Jane Applegate's *201 Great Ideas for Your Small Business*, and I was looking forward to hearing the rest of the tape. Some people might consider it homework, but for me it was pleasure. And then it came to me: I don't have to *make* myself listen to the rest of the tape. It was exactly what I wanted to be doing with my life. It was entertainment, not work.

Years ago, when I was taking courses in textile design at the Fashion Institute of Technology, I loved painting in class, and I loved the homework. But I had to drag myself into Macy's to check out the new fabric designs. I knew that if textile design was truly right for me, browsing stores would be a priority. It wasn't. That was my first clue that maybe it wasn't the right career. I wasn't going to dethrone Laura Ashley.

No matter where I am, I have an audio device with me or a packet of business articles to read. I don't read novels much anymore, to the chagrin of my English-teacher husband. I crave accumulating knowledge about why and how entrepreneurs operate. I'm always listening to a motivational or informational speaker, a downloaded program from National Public Radio, or a CD from the library.

I've always watched what people do more closely than I've listened to what they say. I hold myself to the same test. When I hear myself or anyone else say "I really want to . . . ," I observe to see if there's some behavior to back up that dream. Otherwise, I recognize it as more of a fantasy than a goal.

※　※　※

LESSON 99

At any given moment, you are doing exactly what you choose to be doing, whether you admit it or not.

Talk about wearing your heart on your sleeve—how about the words on people's T-shirts? My friend Marcie Shepard mentioned one T-shirt quotation that was the saddest and funniest I'd ever heard. "I ran out of sick days, so I called in dead." So few words, yet so revealing.

Many years ago, my friend Jerry was working as a short-order cook to support his family until his operatic career took off. For his birthday one year, we were invited to give gag gifts. I embroidered a white chef's apron with the words "I'd rather be singing." It got a laugh even though it broadcast his underlying angst. He wanted a singing career, but at the same time he realized he might not succeed and understood that he had financial obligations to his family.

At first I went into teaching art, rather than doing art, because I had no idea how I could make a living as an artist. I might have claimed that I would rather be painting, but truthfully I knew I would rather be working at a job with a salary, benefits, and paid vacations than figuring out how to survive as an artist. I didn't know how to do that work and was scared.

When I was a full-time mother, I occasionally voiced longings to work outside my home, but if that was what I truly desired, I could have made it happen. My real choice was what I was spending my time doing.

Once I began doing what I love, first as a craft artist, then as a speaker and coach, I wouldn't rather be doing anything else. Yet, I never could have gotten to this point in my entrepreneurial life without passing through all the other stages first.

※　※　※

LESSON 100
The rewards offered by taking a leadership role far outweigh the demands of the position.

My father was vice president of Stern Brothers, a department store in New York City. As daughter of a vice president, I became content to serve as second in command, advising the leader and being the trusted servant. In school I ran for secretary rather than president, stage manager rather than director, helper rather than leader of the troops. I was afraid to bear the full responsibility for being the boss. As long as my superior would take the heat while praising me amply, basking in reflected glory was as much as I could handle.

This is how I changed. The volunteer coordinator at my children's elementary school recognized my artistic talents and asked me to chair the holiday craft and merchandise fair, the biggest fundraising event the school scheduled. She was someone I admired and knew I would enjoy working with. I knew she would support me in the work. So at thirty-three, I said yes to a leadership role for the first time in my life.

I found that I enjoyed being in charge, being the decision maker. When the family room—the area in the building devoted to volunteers— was abuzz with workers preparing products for the fair, I was in my glory. I doled out assignments, supervised quality control, worked on the budget, and dealt with problems. It was my first step toward leadership, but I wouldn't have taken on the job without the coordinator's support.

It took me another year before I took on a leadership role without such clear support. Years of therapy helped me abdicate the role of second banana. I was ready to be the chief. In 1996 I accepted the nomination to become the president of the Entrepreneurial Woman's Network, a 300-member organization.

The yearlong commitment was enormous. I led a board of directors consisting of twenty-four women who owned their own businesses. The work was nonstop, filled with deadlines for workshops, lunches, and round-table meetings. In addition, I wrote a regular column for the organization's newsletter, presided over the monthly membership luncheons, and dealt with all the issues that arose.

What I loved best was the intensity of the job and interacting with people. It made me feel enormously alive, vital. During that year, the media called me frequently for comment. I was invited to attend conferences as a representative of the group. Everyone in the organization knew my name. It was never quite like that when I was the vice president. In that position, I could go and hide. When you're the leader, they come and find you.

Being president that year changed my life and opened up a passion for leadership. I had been president, a claim I could never have made before. And, as long as the Entrepreneurial Woman's Network exists, my name will be listed among the presidents.

※   ※   ※

LESSON 101
Success is enjoying what you've worked hard to get and recognizing you're there.

There were moments in my art studio when every action was conscious: pulling up my e-mail, flipping through my Rolodex, noticing the stack of bills awaiting my attention. Then there were moments when I picked up a stylus, put on my magnifying glasses, reached into an egg carton, and began to make wax markings on the surface of the shell. I was not aware of the time, of my breath, of anything other than the activity of my hands. My attention was on the aroma of the melting beeswax, the heft of the egg in my fingers, and the design unfolding before me. I was, as they say, in the zone.

The same has become true for my speaking and coaching. When I'm on the phone coaching or in front of an audience sharing my knowledge, I am doing work that I love and that is financially rewarding. My office is an environment that I have created in a home I love. And, most important, I recognize that I have created a career that makes me happy. For me, this is success.

Yes, there are moments when a client forgets an appointment, a group doesn't fill, or a blog post fails to attract readers. There are times when piles of paper completely cover my carefully designed workspace, evenings when my husband's long hours at work are preferable to his presence in the house. I am normal.

It takes years to achieve this simplicity and satisfaction. You'll know you're there when you no longer look over your shoulder to see what the other guy is doing, if he's happier than you, or if his house is bigger and his kids have nicer outfits.

Attending a friend's fiftieth birthday party, I met a woman who ran an economic development office in northern New England. She had a difficult time believing her client when she said she'd be happy making $20,000 a year raising and selling her tomatoes. I understood that client exactly. To me, she is the quintessential lifestyle entrepreneur.

That woman and I chose our paths as a means to create a thriving life. We both know exactly what we need to do, and the desire for externals is diminished.

What I have accomplished with my work and life is my own definition of success. I know what I want to be doing. I've gotten to a point in my life where I am doing it. I recognize that I have what I want. As simple as that sounds, I don't know many people who have achieved this.

※　※　※

ACKNOWLEDGEMENTS

Putting together this new edition of *Soul Proprietor: 101 Lessons from a Lifestyle Entrepreneur* has forged deeper relationships with numerous people. Kate Kelly, wondrous client, prolific author and sought-after professional speaker, made me tea one afternoon and talked me through the ins and outs of various publishing venues. Maria Scrivan, one of my favorite creative clients had done extensive research on self-publishing (*Dogi the Yogi*) and generously shared her hours of wisdom in a summarized list. Chris Timmons, fellow Artsy Girl and the first person to even suggest I had a book in me before I wrote *Decorating Eggs*, added to that list and suggested that I use Kim Barron's services for book design. Great suggestion! It was heaven working with Kim. Her tag line is "No ego. No attitude. Just great design." It's true.

Copywriter Jennifer Odear was referred to me by admired colleague Kim DeYoung. Jennifer took the first version of *Soul Proprietor*, tossed it up into the air with all my newsletter and blog articles and magically rearranged it all to make perfect sense.

One of my dearest friends, Doreen Birdsell, wrote her memoir recently. When she asked me about an editor, I called my good friend and writing colleague Susie Haubenstock as a possible referral. Susie declined and passed on Marggie Graves' name to Doreen with happy results. I went right to Marggie when I was at the editing stage of this project. Her joyful encouragement propelled me forward. I owe her so much for her contribution.

Pamela Miles came to me for coaching and then we turned the table because I wanted what she was offering. She makes authors famous. If you're reading this, it's working!

I owe a great deal to Lena West who initiated me into the blogosphere. This brilliantly savvy and patient woman led me with a firm hand and a gentle heart into the new frontier. Not only did she guide me step by step, but she also became a strong advocate for my message. Were it not for Lena, this second edition may never have come to be. Blogging has given me a reason to write. I simply love reporting out the experiences of an entrepreneur. It helped me develop my purpose – to give voice to the heartbeat of soul proprietors everywhere.

Nothing happens in my office without the bedrock support and administrative skills of my virtual assistant Valerie Crowley. Without her, everything else would fall through the cracks. Although we've never met, she is a dear colleague and trusted ally.

Amelia Harris, a fellow (albeit much younger Mount Holyoke College alumna), came to me through my good friend Jessica Bram. Amelia was looking to fill in a few hours a week while searching for a job. It was my good fortune that this occurred right when my book project was getting underway. Amelia personally keystroked the entire manuscript, researched print houses, scoured the Internet for social networking connections and provided a stability and constancy to the work at hand.

There's a small, but hearty contingent of beautifiers out there I'd like to thank. Farah Khan, my graphic designer who became a client, created my newest branding that illustrates her belief in me and my coaching. She recommended Paul Specht to represent a lifestyle image of me through his lens. He photographed me for the cover shot and captured how joyous I feel in my work. Scarlett DeBease, my personal wardrobe stylist, has become a dear friend. As the only person who has been privy to my closet, Scarlett made me look good at countless speaking engagements, networking events and on my book's cover.

I want to thank Rick Fierberg and Nancy Follis for their willingness and even ardor in giving their eagle eye abilities to the proofing of my galley copies. Over the years I've had generous corrections sent to me when typos have appeared in my blog posts or on my website, but something about the integrity and generosity of these two friends makes their contribution to this effort extraordinary in my eyes.

My beloved mastermind group: Mary Ellroy, Valerie Gosset and Brenda Slovin, have seen me through thick and thin. They listened to me procrastinate about starting my blog for months on end. It was they who suggested it originally as a productive forum for me. They were entirely right.

My clients provide the foundation for so many of my lessons. They have always generously allowed me to share the wisdom gained through our work together when asked. I am forever grateful for the privilege and trust this relationship offers.

I refer to the Entrepreneurial Woman's Network over and over again in my book because of the vast impact this organization has had on my career. I've met women who have become my suppliers, colleagues, clients and partners. The institution itself has inspired me and transformed me. I would not be where I am today without having been a member of EWN.

I have been part of an anonymous fellowship for over twenty years now, so naming the incredible supporters I've found in the rooms would be a violation of the traditions. Suffice it to say that there are legions of men and women I thank for their ongoing appreciation, acceptance and unconditional love. Next time we do our secret handshake, know that this acknowledgment is for you.

I want to mention three friends and creative colleagues who have been there for me for over thirty years each and who are more like sisters than friends: Marisabina (Cookie) Russo, Aimee Garn and Linda Carr. These women have become family and I love them so.

Speaking of family I must express my enduring appreciation for my siblings, Meredith Bernstein, Barbara Raho and Andy Goodman, who have seen it all and *still* love and support me.

The greatest testimony to my lifestyle entrepreneurship is the happiness level and success of my three children. One of Laura's first words expressed, while bending over my art space, was "fra-gile." They all learned early what working from home looked like and were respectful and proud of their mom's work. I could not be more thrilled or proud of whom they have become. They are happy in their work and have chosen loving partners. Lindsey, Rob, Laura, Evan and Anne—you're the best!

※ ※ ※

RESOURCES

Dr. Wayne Dyer	http://www.drwaynedyer.com/
Roger Dawson	http://www.rdawson.com/
Entrepreneurial Women's Network	http://www.ewn-ct.org/
Carol Duvall	http://www.hgtv.com/the-carol-duvall-show/video/index.html
Dr. Julie White	http://www.fivestarspeakers.com/espeakers/16123/Julie-White.html
Brian Tracy	http://www.briantracy.com/
Artoria	http://www.artoria.com/index.php
The Artist's Way/Julia Cameron	http://www.theartistsway.com/
Cherie Carter-Scott	http://www.drcherie.com/
Anne Lamott	http://www.barclayagency.com/lamott.html
Victoria Magazine	http://www.victoriamag.com/
The Business of Bliss	http://www.amazon.com/Business-Bliss-Profit-Doing-What/dp/0688160840
Anna Quindlen	http://www.annaquindlen.net/
Mary Ellroy	http://www.gamebird.biz/
Kate White	http://katewhite.com/
Mark Victor Hansen	http://markvictorhansen.com/
How I Got on the Today Show CD	http://www.janepollak.com/book_detail.asp?PageID=1074
Ornament Magazine	http://www.ornamentmagazine.com/
National Speakers Association	http://www.nsaspeaker.org/
Zig Ziglar	http://www.ziglar.com/home.html
Susan Keane Baker	http://www.susanbaker.com/
Paper House Productions	http://www.paperhouseproductions.com/
National Stationery Show	http://www.nationalstationeryshow.com/
Jack Mitchell	http://www.hugyourcustomers.com/
Rick Wetzel	http://www.rickwetzel.com/index.php
Relationship Coaching	http://centerforrightrelationships.com/
Lena West	http://lenawest.com/
Faith Ringgold	http://www.faithringgold.com/

Noel (spa)	http://noelle.com/
Mount Holyoke College	http://www.mtholyoke.edu
Neiman Marcus	http://www.neimanmarcus.com
International Coach Federation	http://www.coachfederation.org/
Dr. Debbie Danowski	http://www.debbiedanowski.com/
Virtual Assistant	http://www.assistu.com/
Dr. Alan Weiss	http://www.summitconsulting.com/
The Coaches Training Institute	http://www.thecoaches.com/
Pedro Boregaard	http://www.boregaard.com/
Flax Art & Design Catalog	http://www.flaxart.com/
Carmine Picarello	http://www.picarellophoto.com/
Nancy Michaels, Impression Impact	http://www.nancymichaels.com/
Country Home Magazine	http://www.countryhome.com/
Service Corps of Retired Executives (SCORE)	http://www.score.org/index.html
Decoration and Design Building	http://www.ddbuilding.com/
Jack Canfield	http://www.jackcanfield.com/
Jane Applegate	http://theapplegategroup.com/index.html
Fashion Institute of Technology	http://www.fitnyc.edu/
Marcie Shepard	http://www.marcieshepardseminars.com/